MW01118267

ZOMBIE BIRDS, ASTRONAUT FISH, *AND OTHER* WEIRD ANIMALS

BECKY CREW
FOUNDER OF *RUNNING PONIES* ON THE
SCIENTIFIC AMERICAN BLOG NETWORK

Adjamsmedia
AVON, MASSACHUSETTS

Published by
Adams Media, a division of F+W Media, Inc.
57 Littlefield Street, Avon, MA 02322. U.S.A.
www.adamsmedia.com

ISBN 10: 1-4405-6026-9
ISBN 13: 978-1-4405-6026-2
eISBN 10: 1-4405-6335-7
eISBN 13: 978-1-4405-6335-5

Printed in the United States of America.

10   9   8   7   6   5   4   3   2   1

Interior illustrations by Di Quick.

*This book is available at quantity discounts for bulk purchases.
For information, please call 1-800-289-0963.*

To Alex
For making me tough when I was tired and brave when I was scared. You give me butterflies.

CONTENTS

PART THREE: ANCIENT CREATURES   111

PART FOUR: PREY   137

PART FIVE: ODD BODIES 183

Introduction

I was standing in the most exquisite living room I had ever seen, disguised in a bear costume that was chafing the hell out of my left thigh. I had been commissioned by an editor acquaintance of mine to report on a rapidly emerging phenomenon known as Animals Anonymous, which, if the rumors were to be believed, was like the most neurotic menagerie ever assembled.

I was instructed to head to the public pool for my first meeting if I was of the aquatic persuasion. I said, "Actually, I'm a bear," so was given directions to the home of a very well-respected Spanish ribbed newt.

The newt had made himself a tidy fortune as a venture capitalist before retiring to a newly acquired Beaux-Arts mansion in the leafy part of town. I only ever saw his living room, complete with walls inlaid with mother-of-pearl, rich antique walnut furniture, and ceiling-to-floor drapes embroidered with 22-carat gold, but it's safe to say this newt is very good at buying houses. Which is fortunate, because all bug-eyed and grayish skinned, he wasn't the most attractive amphibian I'd come across.

"Take a seat, we're about to begin," he told me.

I sank into the nearest armchair, and if beleaguered thighs could breathe a sigh of relief, my left one poured itself a glass of red.

The rest of the attendees took their seats, and soon enough, there were all kinds of frogs and lizards and rodents and birds gathered in groups of three or four on each. There were bats hanging from the drapes and a collection of insects and arachnids peering out from over the rim of a silver tureen. A giant panda eyed me from across the room in a way that made me feel distinctly uncomfortable.

"Eurasian Roller, why don't you start things off?" said the Spanish ribbed newt.

"Okay," a striking gold and turquoise–colored bird replied gloomily. "Hi, I'm Eurasian Roller, and being an animal is ruining my life."

"Hi, Eurasian Roller," the room droned.

"My nest is in a pretty dangerous part of town," she continued, "and I can't come home from a day of foraging without the chicks having thrown up all over the place. They're always getting spooked. All I ever do at home is clean up vomit."

"Is this something that can be treated with therapy?" offered a minuscule, warty toad perched very deliberately on the sheerest edge of its chair.

"No, it's just the curse of our species. I should have sent the damned things to boarding school when I had the chance."

As the night progressed, each animal told its story, ranging from, "My mother insists I eat her and I'm just not sure I'm ready for that," to "There's a pretty good chance I'm going to fuck an empty beer bottle once this meeting is over."

"I'm in heat and I'm the only panda in town," said the giant panda. "I'm only in heat once a year. It's *unbearable*." She never took her eyes off me.

"And what's your story, Mr. . . . ?"

"Ted. And it's Ms.," I said. The giant panda looked away, mortified.

"Terribly sorry, Ms. Ted," said the newt.

"Easy mistake. My fur's always given off an ambiguous vibe, genderwise. I guess that's why my parents left me when I was seventeen months old. I've never really gotten over it."

No one seemed particularly moved by my fabricated confession, particularly the spider who said, "Did you not just hear my story about my mother? The eating . . . ?"

I changed the subject. "Spanish Ribbed Newt, can I ask what your story is?"

His puffy eyes looked suddenly very sad. "I have everything in the world that a male could want, except a mate for life."

All the females in the room sighed wistfully. (At least I think they were females; it was very hard to tell in several species I'd never seen before in my life.)

"Why is that?" I ventured.

The newt removed his spectacles and placed them gently on the arm of his chair. Then, without warning, he violently contorted his torso in such a way that his ribs ripped right through his clammy flesh like a set of gnarly spears. Then he straightened himself out again, which pulled his ribs back inside his tiny frame. "Females can't stand it for more than a couple of months. It's too vile, even for the gold diggers. The situation is so hopeless that I've resorted to online dating. It's not going very well."

A heavily armored lizard was looking very intently at him.

"Well, would you look at the time," said the newt, replacing his spectacles as he attempted to do the same with his dignity. "I'll see you lot at the bar."

"Look, if it's all the same to you I'd rather leave the sunglasses on."

"You didn't have to go drinking with them, you know," my editor told me as I heaved myself into his office the morning after. "Now, let's see what you've got."

"Seriously, I could have just e-mailed the article to you. That way I wouldn't have had to throw up in your—"

"They're just like us! Their body image issues, their family squabbles—even their sex lives!"

"Yeah, that's what I thought. Until a monkey urinated on himself and scored all the dates."

PART ONE

HUNTERS

The Most Powerful Punch on Earth?

PEACOCK MANTIS SHRIMP
(*Odontodactylus scyllarus*)

AT NO MORE THAN 7 inches long, the peacock mantis shrimp is small, but it packs a punch with the acceleration of a .22 caliber bullet.

There are 400 known species in the stomatopod, or "mantis shrimp," group, which contains solitary-living, predatory crustaceans that are technically neither mantis nor shrimp. They are found in tropical and sub-tropical waters, with more than half of all species occurring in the Indo-West Pacific region. They spend their days holed up in burrows or crevices in shallow coral reefs and on the sandy seabed as far as 4920 feet below the surface. The peacock mantis shrimp (*Odontodactylus scyllarus*) is arguably the most beautiful of all the stomatopods, with velvety olive, red, and brilliant turquoise varieties, each with a dual chain of deep red legs and the strangest barely pink eyes. They are distinguished by the spattering of orange leopard spots across the white of their anterior, or frontal, carapace, which, when the peacock mantis shrimp is face on, give it the appearance of an exotic lily.

Mantis shrimp species are grouped according to their hunting techniques. There are the "spearers," with front legs that end in a barbed spike perfect for impaling fish, and the larger "smashers," who thrust their club-shaped claws at speeds of up to 75 feet per second to shatter the protective shells of crabs, clams, and snails.

Even larger prey such as octopuses and clown fish are not safe from the peacock mantis shrimp, and you wouldn't handle one if you were fond of having a complete set of digits. One of the world's top mantis shrimp experts, Roy Caldwell, a professor of integrative biology at the University of California, Berkeley, tells the tale of a South African surgeon who once tried to remove a peacock mantis shrimp from its tank, only to have his finger mangled so badly it required amputation. And several aquariums have had their tanks destroyed by peacock mantis shrimp, a particular individual named Tyson famously smashing through his tank's 0.2-inch-thick glass in 1998. Little Tyson was only 4 inches long.

In 2004, Caldwell and his colleagues got hold of a $60,000 high-speed camera, capable of shooting 100,000 frames per second, to investigate the peacock mantis shrimp's lightning-fast punch. By slowing the action down by a factor of 883, the team discovered that the creature had an odd, saddle-shaped spring within the hinge of the club. Known as a hyperbolic paraboloid, this type of spring arrangement is often used by engineers and architects to reinforce buildings, but is rarely seen in nature. Like a crossbow, it stays locked and compressed while the mantis shrimp's front leg is cocked, which stores elastic energy until the latch is suddenly released as the arm is extended. The spring gives the claw a peak acceleration of 10,000 times the force of gravity, and strike forces that are thousands of times the peacock mantis shrimp's body weight. According to Sheila Patek from Harvard University, a biologist who coauthored the paper with Caldwell in *Nature* that year, the speed of this strike far exceeds most measured animal movements, except that of the trap-jaw ant (*Odontomachus bauri*) of Central and South America.

Patek went on to lead a research team that measured the speed at which this ant snaps shut its mandibles, which are the pair of appendages near its mouth. Using high-speed videography, the researchers clocked the speed at 115–210 feet per second—2300 times faster than the blink of an eye—which they claimed in a 2006 paper in *Proceedings of the National Academy of Sciences* is the fastest self-powered predatory strike in the animal kingdom.

Patek is now investigating the movements of other mantis shrimp species, and thinks the peacock mantis shrimp could have a rival in its own family. "Each species has different strike features—some are faster and some are much slower," she says. "And, although we haven't published it yet, we have found another mantis shrimp species that may be even more impressive than the peacock mantis shrimp."

Patek and Caldwell's team also found that the peacock mantis shrimp's punch was particularly destructive due to a process known as cavitation. Its superfast strike lowers the pressure in the water surrounding the point of impact, causing it to boil and produce exploding bubbles. While emitting a loud clicking noise, and sometimes even flashes of bright light, these bubbles will soften the hard shells of sea snails and clams when they explode, making it easier for the peacock mantis shrimp to break through its prey's armored exterior.

Poor Peacock Mantis Shrimp. With a punch like that, he's going to have a hard time convincing the entire ocean that he's not a total psychopath. One night he'll be at home, quietly ironing and watching something with Gordon Ramsay in it, when a pair of unexpected visitors will turn up on his doorstep.

"Yes?"

Two starfish in police uniforms will invite themselves inside, drink a cup of his very expensive tea and tell him they've both seen this episode already and how great is Gordon Ramsay?

"Yeah, I know. That's why I'm watching it."

"Anyway," they'll say, "you're the main suspect in the murder of a crab whose mashed-up remains were found in a garbage bin behind the gym tonight."

"What? I don't murder crabs, I buy my crab meat from the supermarket, like everyone else," Peacock Mantis Shrimp will tell them, but he'll end up in court the next day anyway.

The two starfish in police uniforms will have to cross-examine him, because there's no such thing as lawyers under the ocean. (There's no such thing as a justice system under the ocean either, so the fact that they managed to cobble together some semblance of a courtroom in the space of twenty-four hours will be something of a minor miracle. And I do mean minor, because it might *look* like a proper courtroom, but that doesn't mean that anyone inside it will know what the hell they're supposed to be doing.)

"So, Mr. Peacock Mantis Shrimp, can you please tell the court exactly what you did on the night of August 5?"

"I told you! I ironed, watched some TV, made a sandwich . . . then the two of you barged in and drank all my tea."

A very uncomfortable-looking blue cod in a wig will be sitting on the bench, furiously scribbling something in his notepad before crossing it out again with long, hopeless strokes.

"Tell us about this sandwich you made, Mr. Peacock Mantis Shrimp."

"It was just lettuce and crab meat—"

"*Crab meat . . . ?*" the two starfish in police uniforms will repeat suggestively, swiveling around to give the jury the starfish equivalent of a raised eyebrow.

"Yes, I got it from the supermarket—"

"Do you have an alibi, Mr. Peacock Mantis Shrimp?"

"No, I'm a stomatopod. I live alone."

"Indeed."

The courtroom will erupt into a chorus of anxious murmurs and the blue cod judge will mutter to no one in particular that he has no idea what he's doing.

The head jury member, an eel, will stand up.

"Down in front!" One of the other jury members will instruct.

"No, idiot, he's supposed to do that!" the two exasperated starfish in police uniforms will respond, doing whatever the starfish equivalent of burying their heads in their hands is. "Mr. Eel, have you reached a decision?"

"Yes. We think you *should* reimburse Mr. Peacock Mantis Shrimp for his tea."

"What? We're not on trial here! *He* is!"

But Peacock Mantis Shrimp will have punched a hole through the courthouse wall and he'll be halfway to the train station before the two starfish in police uniforms even figure out what just happened. So we can all stop feeling sorry for him now, he's got this well under control.

Not only can the peacock mantis shrimp throw one hell of a punch, it also has the most sophisticated eyes of any animal in the world. Like flies, honeybees, and praying mantises, the mantis shrimp has a pair of compound eyes made up of many different facets. The surface consists of two hemispheres separated by a midband, and all three sections are capable of viewing an object independently of each other. This is known as trinocular vision, and it is far superior to the binocular vision humans have, because we need to use both of our eyes simultaneously to achieve the best result.

The mantis shrimp's midband is separated into six rows of ommatidia, which are structures that carry a cluster of light-sensitive cells called photoreceptors. The first four rows of ommatidia contain specific types of photoreceptors that respond to different wavelengths of light, allowing the mantis shrimp to see in both the infrared and ultraviolet range. Special filters allow each photoreceptor to respond to changing light conditions in the area. The fifth and sixth rows contain photoreceptors that can detect different planes of polarized light, according to a 2008 *Current Biology* study led by biologist Tsyr-Huei Chiou from the University of Maryland. Nonpolarized light is the kind that comes from the sun and is visible to humans, and it is made up of electromagnetic waves that oscillate in a direction perpendicular to the way the light is traveling. If this direction is restricted, for example, if nonpolarized light is made to pass through a particular type of crystal or reflected off the surface of water, the oscillations will be forced to point in the same direction that the light is traveling. This produces a particular form called linear polarized light, which appears as nothing more than a bright glare to the human eye.

The mantis shrimp is the only type of animal known to detect another type of polarized light called circular polarized light (CPL), which is produced under the water where linear polarized light is scattered as it heads toward the surface. Chiou found that three species of mantis shrimp have shells that can reflect CPL, which causes them to change color. He suggested that the function of this could be that of a "secret communication channel," allowing courting individuals to send sexual signals to each other without attracting the attention of predatory squids and octopuses that are unable to perceive the reflections.

In mid-2011, researchers from Penn State University described in *Nature Communications* how their investigation into the visual mechanisms of the peacock mantis shrimp helped them to invent two-part waveplate technology that could improve CD, DVD, Blu-ray, and holographic technology. And elsewhere, researchers are working to improve the CPL filters used in both ordinary and high-tech medical photography by gaining a better understanding of just how the most incredible eyes in the world operate.

A Mouse in Wolf's Clothing

A KEEN HUNTER WITH a penchant for howling at the moon, the northern grasshopper mouse is a true wolf in sheep's clothing. One of three species in the grasshopper mouse family, this strictly nocturnal, stout-bodied rodent hails from the drier regions of North America between central Canada and northern Mexico, stealing burrows from prairie dogs and kangaroo rats by day and hunting by night.

With 70–90 percent of its diet consisting of animal material, the northern grasshopper mouse is one of the most highly carnivorous rodents in the world, regularly making a meal out of prey as tough as tarantulas, scorpions, and other rodents. They grow to around 5–7 inches long, have clublike tails, and are wrapped in dense, silky coats of warm cinnamon or grey with undersides of white. The northern grasshopper mouse's coloring may give it a rather sweet appearance, but this mouse was born to kill, with long claws for scratching and grasping onto its prey. And unlike most rodents, it has enlarged jaw muscles for a greater bite force, and its molars are specialized for puncturing and slicing through hard insect carapaces and flesh.

Although primarily wanderers, northern grasshopper mice can maintain unusually large territories of around 6 acres each, and they will defend them aggressively. Researchers suspect this is what has led to their incredible calling behavior. Described in 1929 by biologists Vernon Bailey and Charles Sperry as "a long, fine, shrill whistle given in a high key—a wolf howl in miniature," and again by Bailey in 1931 as "similar to the hunting call of a timber wolf" the howl of the northern grasshopper mouse is as chilling as it is distinct. Later, in 1966, David Ruffer from Defiance College in Ohio wrote in the *Ohio Journal of Science* that these extremely vocal rodents appeared to have not one, but four distinct calls:

(1) a squeak call emitted by animals less than four days old and by adults during some fights; (2) a high-pitched, chirping call—ech, ech, ech, ech—was an alarm note given by individuals during an intense fight or when they were being removed from a cage; (3) a high-pitched, piercing call which lasted 0.8 seconds (mean of 183 records); and (4) a call similar to type three, but broken so that it sounded like two shortened type-three calls, one immediately following the other, and lasting 0.9 seconds (mean of 71 records).

Ruffer suggested that the third call was a kind of communication between grasshopper mice of the same species, describing how his captive mice would emit this particular call when placed alone in an enclosure, and the longer they were left there, the less frequent it became. The fourth call, on the other hand, was made only when the captive mouse had been made aware of the presence of another grasshopper mouse of either sex, but was unable to find or make contact with it. Remarkably, occasionally when a northern grasshopper mouse is making either call three or four, it will mimic the posture of a wolf, throwing its little head back to point its nose to the sky and howl.

More recently, the northern grasshopper mouse has gained an unfortunate reputation as a carrier of the plague caused by *Yersinia pestis*—the bacterium that caused the Black Death, which wiped out 200 million Europeans in the fourteenth century. Over the past few decades *Y. pestis* has decimated five species of prairie dog across North America. For years, researchers were bewildered that a prairie dog population could be completely obliterated by the plague within months, and when another population moved into the vacant burrows, it too would be wiped out by the same disease. How could the plague persist so strongly after the original, infected colony is already gone?

According to James Holland Jones, associate professor of anthropology at Stanford University and coauthor of a paper published in *Proceedings of the Royal Academy of Sciences* in mid-2011, the pathogen could be getting into the soil to infect the recolonized prairie dog town. Alternatively, it might be carried by a carnivore such as the northern grasshopper mouse, Jones suggested. Prairie dog families, or coteries, live together in well-defined territories that they know not to venture out of, which should theoretically confine the plague within rigid boundaries. But northern grasshopper mice do not respect the prairie dog territories and appear to carry plague fleas from family to family, spreading the disease further and faster than ever before.

"And now the best man, Roger, will give his toast. Oh, and the caterers would like to apologize for completely underestimating just how much everyone here loves fruitcake. Who would have thought? They also said to tell you that they have a stack of spare fruit platters . . . Okay, okay, I know it's not the same, you don't have to boo me, jeez . . ."

"Thanks, Mike. Hey don't egg him, he's family! Ha, kidding! I'm kidding. I barely know the guy. Anyway . . . We've had some good times, Martin and me. I'll never forget that prank we pulled on those prairie dogs that one time. Poor bastards. We must have killed off, what, fifty, sixty of them in just a couple of weeks? Martin was so good at it, he'd stroll up to their burrows, all, 'I have an extremely important announcement to make on behalf of the Small Mammals of America Association, you need to gather everyone in the common room immediately!' So the prairie dogs packed themselves in real tight and Martin rubbed himself on each of them, like, 'It's cool, this is just how grasshopper mice say hello.' And then he'd get up on the podium, unfurl what was supposed to be his very important announcement before telling them, 'Oh, wait. Oh. Well this is embarrassing. It says "deliver this announcement to the prairie *hogs*." Hogs! I've never even *heard* of prairie hogs before. Anyway, sorry for wasting your time, I'll see myself out.' "

"Oh and then this other time, we're at the pub and Martin's *super* drunk, he's like, 'If only we could kill off Kate's parents so easily.' Ha! What, too far? Okay, okay, I'm done. I'm sitting! I'm sitting. Hey, who ate my fruitcake?"

Birds Coming for Your Brains...

GREAT TIT
(*Parus major*)

"I have a question: How come the *more* brains we eat, the dumber we become? The less capable of holding a conversation? The less interested in laundering our clothes and going to work?"

"Braaaaains . . ."

"I mean, we used to talk about books, and politics, and now it's all just . . ."

"Braaaaains . . ."

"Exactly! Maybe things aren't as bad as—"

"Braaaaains . . ."

"Nope, never mind."

EXTREME HUNGER MIGHT MAKE figurative monsters of us all, but that's nothing compared to what happens when a pretty olive and yellow bird called the great tit suffers a particularly lean winter.

Tits are a family of birds known for their ingenious behavior. In the British Isles during the 1940s, when milkmen still delivered their milk in glass bottles to residents' doorsteps, it was reported that a population of blue tits had figured out how to pry open the aluminum milk caps to get to the fresh layer of cream on the surface. And more recently, bat ecologists Péter Estók and Björn

Siemer from the Max Planck Institute for Ornithology in Germany discovered that great tits (*Parus major*) in Hungary had secured themselves a similarly unexpected meal source.

Great tits are a species of passerine (perching) bird found all over Europe, the Middle East, central and northern Asia, and some regions of North Africa. They are a large species of tit, at 4.9–5.5 inches in length, with a distinctive black crown, neck, and throat, white cheeks, and subtle olive wings that sit on a lemon-yellow breast.

Having observed a single great tit hunt a tiny species of bat called the common pipistrelle (*Pipistrellus pipistrellus*) in the Bükk Mountains of northeast Hungary in the winter of 1996, Estók set out ten years later to determine whether this was a one-off event, or something the great tits in the area did regularly. He watched more than fifty Hungarian great tits over two winters, discovering that they had taught each other how to use the waking call of pipistrelles emerging from hibernation to track them down, wrench them from their cave roosts, and crack open their skulls to feed on their brains. After entering the cave the great tits needed no more than fifteen minutes to capture a groggy bat, and in some cases were observed carrying the bats out of the cave to be eaten in nearby trees. Publishing in a 2009 issue of *Biology Letters*, Estók reported that he and Siemer had identified a case of cultural transmission occurring in these birds, where a specific behavior is learned between individuals and passed on through generations.

As part of their research, Estók and Siemer played a recording of the waking bat calls to the group of great tits they had collected from the wild, finding that the noise attracted around 80 percent of them toward the speakers. This was an odd result, they said, because previous studies of bat calls had seen this same chatter drive birds away. They also tempted the great tits with bacon bits and sunflower seeds at the same time as playing the pipistrelle calls to see which they preferred. They found that the great tits preferred the bacon and seeds, which are similar to their usual diet of berries and insects, suggesting that their zombie-esque behavior was motivated by necessity during unusually harsh winters.

The Sock-Loving Vampire Spider

WHILE GREAT TITS ARE only part-time zombies, there's a species of spider that's a full-blown vampire.

A little Kenyan jumping spider called *Evarcha culicivora*, otherwise known as the vampire spider, has been found to have a serious case of bloodlust, feeding off it and fueling its sex life with it. The 0.2-inch-long, black, white, and crimson species was discovered in 2003 by biologist Robert Jackson from the University of Canterbury in New Zealand, who has been studying its peculiar habits ever since. One of his investigations revealed *E. culicivora* as the only predator that chooses its prey based on what its prey has eaten. Which is where humans come in: The vampire spider's preferred prey is mosquitoes, and the sooner it can make a meal out of a mosquito that has made a meal out of one of us, the happier *E. culicivora* is.

Jackson and colleagues tested the ability of these spiders to pick a mosquito that has just fed over a mosquito that hasn't, plus which option—blood filled or regular—they preferred. Because only female mosquitoes are equipped to siphon out and feed on mammalian blood, the researchers presented the spiders with a number of food options, including male mosquitoes. In 2005, they reported in *Proceedings of the National Academy of Sciences* that *E. culicivora* chose the blood-filled female mosquitoes over all other kinds of prey 83 percent of the time, and the spiders could pick their favorite kind of mosquito using either sight or smell with a success rate of 90 percent. Great sight is a rare ability in spiders, as those who live in webs can simply wait for their prey to come to them, using vibrations to detect their whereabouts. Webless jumping spiders, on the other hand, rely on keen senses to actively seek out their meals—and what a good meal blood is, because there's no preparation required, no energy-hungry process of liquefying with digestive enzymes. It's ready-made and full of nutrients.

Of course, finding and catching mosquitoes that have just fed but haven't yet fully digested their meal is no easy feat, and researchers think this difficulty could explain why *E. culicivora* are more attractive to each other if they smell like blood. "This diet might be more difficult to satisfy, and it's possible that after eating a blood-carrying mosquito, individuals not only smell good because they smell like the preferred prey, but also because they can show a potential mate that they are capable of finding, and catching, this unusual prey," says Fiona Cross, an animal behavior postdoctoral fellow from the University of Canterbury, who joined Jackson to investigate the aphrodisiac potential of blood for these spiders.

In 2009, Jackson and Cross tested the mate preference of *E. culicivora* by wafting the scents of spiders that had either fed on blood-filled mosquitoes, sugar-filled mosquitoes, male (therefore with no blood) mosquitoes, or lake flies. They found that only spiders fed with blood-filled mosquitoes were deemed attractive by both the male and female spiders, suggesting that this was perhaps driven by the assumption that they would pass good hunting skills on to their offspring. "*E. culicivora* has a very weird connection between diet and attraction to the opposite sex," Cross marvels. "It appears that it doesn't simply prefer blood-carrying mosquitoes for nutrition alone. In fact, the more I learn about these spiders the more I realize just how complex they really are. Blood really makes these spiders go quite crazy."

Unlike most jumping spider species, where the males are more active in the courtship process than the females, with *E. culicivora* both sexes are actively involved in courtship and mate selection. This means the blood diet is important to both sexes in attracting a mate, and Cross found that whether male or female, if an individual has to switch to a nonblood diet such as midges—known as "lake flies" in Kenya—for even one day, they appear to render themselves less attractive.

The idea of lustful, blood-sucking vampire spiders has probably creeped you out enough already, but this story only gets worse with the discovery in early 2011 that *E. culicivora* is attracted to our smelly, sweaty socks. If you're sweating anywhere near these tiny predators they will hunt you down, because what better way to locate blood-filled mosquitoes than to follow the source?

Cross and Jackson tested this attraction by wafting the scent of human socks into test tubes containing *E. culicivora*. The spiders were free to leave the test tubes at any stage, which helped the researchers to determine their levels of attraction to the sock scent. Publishing in *Biology Letters,* they described how the spiders were more likely to remain in their test tubes if the scent had come from a sock worn for 12 hours beforehand than from a fresh, unworn sock. Whether male, female, or juvenile, *E. culicivora* remained 15–30 minutes longer if they smelled the scent of smelly socks. "*E. culicivora* is often found around buildings occupied by people. It seems that they are used to being around people. We also noticed that *E. culicivora* is more 'relaxed' around us; when we run experiments, they behave a lot more calmly than other species do," says Cross. "Unfortunately for us, though, some mosquitoes are *also* found around buildings occupied by people. Perhaps being around people is better for *E. culicivora* for finding this unusual prey. Perhaps human odor assists the spider in finding blood-carrying mosquitoes in particular. We don't know this yet, but it begs investigation!"

Now, this story isn't all bad, because these blood-loving spiders show a preference for the female *Anopheles*, the mosquito genus that can carry malaria, so researchers in Kenya are investigating the potential of using *E. culicivora* in the fight against the disease. "*E. culicivora* may be a weird, and complex, animal, but malaria is an even more complicated beast. There is no single magic bullet out there that can, or will, wipe out malaria," says Cross. "However . . . *E. culicivora* comes from the very part of the world where malaria is so serious. Unlike various other methods used for controlling malaria (for example, baited mosquito traps), *E. culicivora* freely lives in this habitat. Why not learn more about this weird, and remarkable, little animal?"

"I am melancholy," I wrote, because it seemed like the appropriate thing to do. "What good are the opportunities awarded by eternal life if all I do, day in, day out, is watch the young grow old, the old wither away, and the—"

Blast. "What is it, Grul?"

"I have your supper ready, sir."

"What is it?"

"Ants, sir."

"Damn it, Grul! I told you I can only have blood from now on! Were you even listening to me? Just throw them away."

"As you wish. Shall I make up your coffin, sir?"

"No, leave me. I'm feeling melancholy."

"Very well, sir."

I came to the realization that I was a vampire almost twelve months earlier. I had been visiting the little town of Dawnhold on business when I met a curious gentleman sitting alone in the corner of an old bar with thick velvet curtains that cordoned off a series of intimate rooms with rich, green potted palms and purple tapestries lined with golden wool. The man was inscrutable. He sat staring at the densely decorated rug upon which his table sat, and appeared to be studying the grotesque, snarling tigers woven into the fabric. I approached him with all the courage I had just drunk at the bar with a bloody steak.

"Marvelous beasts, aren't they?" I remarked, gesturing at the rug with my glass of rye.

"You have no idea," said the man, addressing his untouched glass of deep red wine in a dreary, yet unmistakably ominous, tone.

"You've seen one?"

"I've seen *everything*," he told me, exasperated, pained, and intensely bored all at once.

"That explains why you're not scared of spiders!"

The man gave his wine glass a withering look.

I offered one of my free legs to him. "My name is Pavenic. I'm an art dealer on my way to Mooreth."

"I know who you are. And I know that you're no ordinary spider." He was ignoring my outstretched leg.

"You do?"

"My name is Farkaskoltus, I am a vampire, and I am 4000 years old. I think you should take a seat."

That night I stood in the bathroom doorway of my hotel room, willing myself to go in. "Just go in, regard yourself in the mirror, and put an end to all this nonsense. You're not a vampire, you're just a normal spider." But

I knew it was fruitless. I wasn't a normal spider. I've never been a normal spider, because of the blood.

The next morning I postponed my trip and retreated home. At my request, Grul strung black, floor-length curtains across every window, never to be drawn. It was a miracle, said Farkaskoltus, that I'd survived the sunlight for so long. I isolated myself from the rest of the village, because that seemed like the appropriate thing to do.

"Sir, the mayor has left something for you. A gift, in return for the generous donation you made to the hospital after their entire blood supply *went missing* . . ."

"I know you're trying to make me feel guilty, Grul, but it won't work. Let me see that."

The gift was wrapped in an ornately embroidered handkerchief made of cotton the color of antique ivory with brilliant maroon lace around its edges. I gently peeled away the edges to reveal a silver eggcup with a delicate golden rim. It was so highly polished, I could actually *see* myself in it. "Good *God*!" The eggcup tumbled to the floor and rolled smoothly under a nearby armchair. "Is that what I look like now? Wait, why do I have a reflection? What the devil's going on here? Could Farkaskoltus have been a simple con artist?"

"That would explain why he insists you send your monthly Vampire League membership fee directly to him, sir."

"So I'm not really a vampire spider after all. I'm just a normal spider. I'm *just* a normal spider." It had well and truly dawned on me. I was just a normal spider. "Grul, I'm melancholy."

"If it's any consolation, sir, you'll always be a vampire as far as the villagers are concerned."

"That's true, Grul. Good point."

So Grul and I strapped a drained and headless corpse to one of my dappled mares and sent it down the hill to the village square. It seemed like the appropriate thing to do.

A Slime-Wielding Predator

Dear Manager

I am writing in response to your accusation that I left your establishment on Saturday night without paying for my meal. If I *had* eaten my meal, I would have paid you for it, but as several witnesses will tell you, I never once opened my mouthparts. If I knew how my meal disappeared like that, I would tell you. But I don't.

Please find enclosed your unpaid bill, which I trust you will refrain from sending me in the future.

Yours sincerely

Hagfish

CLEAR CONTENDER FOR UGLIEST creature in the world, the hagfish is one of the only surviving jawless vertebrates in the world, unchanged since its ancestors slunk around the ocean between 530 and 300 million years ago. Long thought to be sedate scavengers, researchers have recently unmasked these primitive, eyeless "snot eels" as skilled, slime-wielding hunters.

Though technically classified as a vertebrate (an animal with a backbone), the hagfish is so primitive that its backbone is nothing more than a flexible rod of tissue cells called a notochord. Hagfish are found all over the world, at depths of between 165 and 2300 feet below sea level, trawling the bottom of the ocean for carrion and other decaying food scraps. If a hagfish is lucky enough to come across a sizeable carcass it will ensconce itself inside, and rather than nibble at it with its mouthparts, it will absorb the nutrients directly through its skin.

In early 2011, researchers led by physiologist Chris Glover from the School of Biological Sciences at the University of Canterbury in New Zealand discovered this phenomenon by watching what happened when two types of radioactively labeled amino acids were applied to multiple pieces of hagfish skin and gills. Publishing in *Proceedings of the Royal Society B,* the team described how the amino acids passed easily through the outer layers of the skin and gills, which is often seen in invertebrates (animals without backbones) such as jellyfish, corals, and sea stars, but never in another vertebrate. This is because vertebrates need to regulate their internal environment, which is why we humans have such impermeable skin. But somehow the hagfish has evolved in such a way that it can cope with serious changes to its internal chemistry.

The researchers suggested that this could be because the hagfish represents a transitional state between the simple feeding mechanisms of aquatic invertebrates and the more specialized and complex digestive systems of aquatic vertebrates. So by absorbing its food through its skin, the hagfish could be demonstrating how it is a combination of vertebrate and invertebrate characteristics, its bizarre eating behavior a reminder of how little it has changed in millions upon millions of years.

Although they weigh only 5 ounces, hagfish can each produce over 5 gallons of slime in a matter of minutes. They are covered in a collection of slime glands that are connected to two rows of 90–200 pores that run down the full length of their bodies. When threatened, the hagfish will excrete huge amounts of mucins, which are slimy, gel-like secretions bonded together with protein threads that expand the instant they come in contact with seawater. To avoid being smothered by its own cloud of goo, the hagfish will twist its body into an overhand knot and slide through itself, wiping itself clean as it escapes.

Researchers have long assumed that the purpose of the hagfish's ability to produce such copious amounts of slime was to defend itself against gilled predators, because some captive hagfish had been accidentally blocking their own gills with it and suffocating. Using underwater cameras set up off the coast of Great Barrier Island in New Zealand, a team of researchers, led again by Glover, obtained video footage of this occurring in the wild for the first time. They reported in a mid-2011 issue of *Nature* that the "slime secreted by hagfishes fills the mouth and gill chamber of their predators, acting as a very rapid (<0.4 sec[ond]) and effective defense mechanism. The predators convulsed their gill arches dramatically in a gagging-type effort to clear the slime from their gill chambers."

The video footage showed an array of species being overwhelmed by hagfish slime, including sharks and bony fishes. Each time, the hagfish would remain where it was, unharmed, while the predator moved away, gagging. Because they can only refer to what they can see in the video footage, the researchers are not sure whether these predators eventually died due to suffocation from the slime, or survived because the slime dissolved in the water soon after.

What the researchers didn't expect to see in their video footage was hagfish actively hunting their prey. One species—the slender hagfish (*Nemamyxine elongata Richardson*)—actually chased a red bandfish into its seafloor burrow and grabbed it with its twin rows of teeth, called toothplates. When the hagfish emerged from the burrow the bandfish was incapacitated, and the researchers suggested that it could well have been slimed. Not bad for one of the most primitive marine vertebrates on Earth.

The Spider-Eating Spider

PALPIMANUS SPIDER
(*Palpimanus gibbulus* and *Palpimanus orientalis*)

"What'll it be, sir? Are you interested in any of our specials this evening?"

"I think I'll just have the spider, thanks."

"No, I said 'what'll *it* be'."

"I know. I said I want the spider."

"But sir, *you're* a spider . . ."

"Do you mind keeping it dow—never mind, everyone's looking now. It's cool, everyone, I'm not a cannibal, I'm just getting a beer."

"A beer? You didn't order a beer. But if you want a beer, I can get you a beer—"

"Just give me a Whale Ale."

"—to wash down that cannibal meal you just ordered. Sicko."

THEY'RE THE SPIDERS OTHER spiders should be terrified of. Not only are the species *Palpimanus gibbulus* and *Palpimanus orientalis* built to battle spiders up to twice their size, but their stealthy patience and ninja-fast moves are the perfect combination for turning the hunter into the hunted.

These two species belong to the *Palpimanus* family, which includes about 100 species of elusive spiders that all have huge, strong forelegs, which are kept raised while the spider is walking. *P. orientalis* and *P. gibbulus* are the only spider-eating *Palpimanus* spiders, and they are found in Mediterranean countries such as Portugal, Spain, and Israel. Told apart only by the shape of their sex organs, this fearsome duo sport bright red, heavily armored abdomens and rich, brown cephalothoraxes, the area that combines the head and the thorax. Both species are extremely rare and nocturnal, so it wasn't until February 2011 that researchers from the Czech Republic discovered exactly how they executed their hunt. "Ten years ago, I went to Israel to the Negev desert . . . and I came across a number of these peculiar spiders. With their huge forelegs they looked like wrestlers," says lead researcher Stano Pekár, an assistant professor from the Institute of Botany and Zoology at Masaryk University. "A colleague told me that these are supposed to feed on other spiders. So I performed first feeding trials and [then] observed their behavior, which was very strange. I found that they refuse most other prey but spiders."

Catching over 150 individuals, the researchers dropped them in a box with another spider species and watched what happened through the lens of a high-speed camera. Once a *Palpimanus* spider recognized its prey, it moved very slowly toward it, forelegs raised. When it was about half a body length away it stopped dead still, legs up, ready to strike. The moment the prey decided to move, the *Palpimanus* spider would lunge at it, grabbing at its body with its forelegs and biting it with its fanglike chelicerae. It would manage all of this in the space of 0.2 seconds. Once the prey was overcome, the *Palpimanus* spider would wrap it up in silk and start feeding on it. In 90 percent of Pekár's trials, the two species of *Palpimanus* spiders managed to successfully overcome their prey, and in the other 10 percent of trials they were captured by rival spiders.

The researchers had a close look at the *Palpimanus* spiders' legs under an electron microscope, discovering that every inch of these species works to ensure they are the perfect predators. Each leg ends with a dense pad of 1500 hairs, called scopulae, which allow the spiders to grip their prey using the same force that allows all species of spiders to climb walls. When Pekár covered the pads in paraffin wax, the spiders' success rate fell so drastically that instead of needing an average of 1.4 tries to catch a meal, they needed 5.9.

In the wild, these spider-eating spiders don't have the benefit of an enclosed space alone with their prey, which can often successfully outrun them. For this reason, the researchers think the *Palpimanus* spiders target so-called retreat-dwelling spiders that hole themselves up in burrows and silk cocoons. If the only exit is suddenly blocked by a *Palpimanus* spider, there's not much a retreat-dwelling spider can do to get away, except inflict a lethal bite. Which won't do them much good either, because both *P. orientalis* and *P. gibbulus* are protected by a layer of cuticle that is twice as thick as the cuticle worn by other spiders on their front halves, and five times as thick on their back halves.

But despite their tough exterior, these *Palpimanus* spiders aren't particularly aggressive. "These spiders are indeed very calm," says Pekár. "For most of the day they sit motionless under rock and come out only at night. When they come across a web or a retreat, they invade it and aim to catch the spider. If the spider escapes, they wait patiently . . . for its return."

These are not the only known spider-eating spiders. *Portia* is a genus of spider-eating jumping spider that includes seventeen species found in tropical forests everywhere from Africa, Australia, China, Malaysia, Nepal, and the Philippines. *Portia* spiders don't have thick armor, massive forelegs, and hairy pads, so they rely far more on strategy than sheer brawn. They wait until their prey is distracted by food before attacking, or using cryptic stalking to disguise their approach, twanging the silk of a prey's web to imitate struggling prey or the courtship signals of a mate.

Portia spiders have proven themselves to be intelligent hunters in laboratory experiments, performing unusually well in a number of problem-solving tasks. White-mustached Portia spiders (*Portia labiata*) have been named one of the smartest animals in the world for their uncanny ability to learn from previous experience, remembering the rhythmic patterns that work to capture the spider species that they have encountered before. They are also incredibly patient planners, sitting and waiting for hours if they miss their prey, knowing that it will return to a particular spot.

A Mind-Controlling Parasite

GREEN-BANDED BROODSAC
(Leucochloridium paradoxum)

"Hey man, let's go shopping, you're low on Doritos."

"I just bought you an entire packet yesterday! Fine, okay, but can you please tell me when you plan on moving out of my stalks? I get that this is nature and sometimes some of us have to deal with having parasites, but, I don't know. I feel like I'm going crazy or something, like you're doing something to my brai—Hey, there's a bird, let's go say hi."

YOU'D BE HARD-PRESSED TO find an organism more despicable than the helminth. These wormlike creatures, also known as flatworms, are defined by their ability to live inside and feed off living hosts, stripping them of their nutrients and wreaking havoc on their digestive systems. While we humans (and our pets) have to worry about helminths such as roundworms, hookworms, and whipworms, which make homes in our intestines through contaminated water or soil, snails and birds face the terrifying prospect of an encounter with the green-banded broodsac.

First discovered in Germany, the green-banded broodsac maintains an incredible lifestyle. As with all life cycles, it can be pretty difficult to decide where to start, but when you're talking about flatworms, a pile of shit seems pretty apt. Ranging from northern to central Europe, the green-banded broodsac lays its eggs in bird feces, which a species of small, amber-colored snail called *Succinea putris* promptly eats. Luckily for the green-banded broodsac, the snail cannot digest these eggs, so once in the snail's digestive system, the broodsacs hatch into free-swimming larvae called miracidia.

Not content to spend its days inside a lowly snail, the green-banded broodsac sets its sights on a grander home—a mansion with wings. While inside the snail's stomach, the larvae use their tiny, fiberlike structures called cilia to move from the snail's stomach to its eyestalks. Here the larvae will morph into a more advanced form of larvae and then team up in hundreds to create long, living tubes called sporocytes. The sporocytes not only give the snail's eyestalks a colorful appearance, but they also hinder the snail's eyesight and override its preference for dark environments in order to make it more visible to the green-banded broodsac's original host.

Once the parasitized snail stumbles out of the darkness, unable to see that it is now in danger of being spotted by predators, the light causes the sporocytes to twitch and pulsate, giving the eyestalks the appearance of two juicy caterpillars. A passing bird will spot the infected stalks and tear them from the snail's head, ingesting the broodsac larvae in the process. At this stage the larvae will transform once again, this time into adult flatworms, while the snail is left to die or be reinfected. The adult flatworms will breed at a rapid rate inside the bird's digestive system, producing hundreds of eggs that will end up in the bird's droppings. And so the sickening life cycle of the green-banded broodsac is complete.

I hope you weren't eating just now.

Isopod Got Your Tongue?

TONGUE-EATING ISOPOD
(*Cymothoa exigua*)

IN 1983, A NEW species was discovered that is literally your worst nightmare if you're a fish. Known as the tongue-eating isopod, this parasitic crustacean belongs to a group including woodlice and pill bugs, whose ancestors date to at least 300 million years ago. There are over 4000 species of isopods living in the world's oceans, and they make a living out of parasitizing other animals, but none go to the extreme lengths of the tongue-eating isopod to ensure a life-time of easy meals.

In 2009, a tongue-eating isopod was discovered inside a type of large fish called a weever by fishermen off the Minquiers, near the Island of Jersey in the English Channel. This 0.8-inch-long buglike parasite had burrowed into the fish through its gills, attached itself to the muscular base of the tongue and sucked the blood from it until it withered away to nothing. Grasping the inside of the fish's mouth, the isopod plays the part of a replacement tongue, feeding off the scraps of food that enter its mouth. This is the only known case of a parasitic animal being able to replace a host organ so effectively.

Not surprisingly, these sinister little freeloaders are prone to bizarre sex lives, too. Not much is known about the sexual behavior of tongue-eating isopods because they are extremely rare, but scientists believe that a juvenile attaches itself to the gills of a fish to begin the process of becoming sexually mature, causing it to morph into the male form. As the young male isopod develops, reaching up to 0.4 inches in length, it can morph again into the female form. If a male cannot find himself a female to mate with—which they'll also do on the gills of a fish—he will simply change sexes and mate with the more available sex.

Now, Weeverfish, this situation can go either way, depending on how well you treat your new houseguest. It's your isopod, you can do whatever you want with it, but if you want my advice, you should probably make the most of things because that isopod isn't going anywhere in a hurry. I'm sure he'd be more than happy to pay a little for his keep in return for you not swishing a mouthful of nails around him like you did when he ate too much of your breakfast that one time.

You know that cute lady weeverfish whom you like but you're always too shy to talk to? Well, your isopod will probably think she's gross because he has very complicated sexual preferences, so you guys could totally do the old, "Why don't you tell me what to say to the boy/girl I like because you're so eloquent and/or suave and I'm so stupid and/or shy and s/he will totally fall in love with me, thinking I'm the eloquent and/or suave one?" thing. It'll be so much easier than when most awkward lovers try it because your isopod won't have to hide in a clump of nearby seaweed or behind a bookshelf and try to whisper to you over an unreasonable distance. What a great team you could make!

On the other hand, you could be a whiny bitch about the whole situation and every time you run into someone and they ask you how you are, you're like, "An isopod replaced my tongue. How do you think I am?" Isopods have feelings too, Weeverfish, and you don't want yours to get upset, because one day you could be in the photocopying room with that woman from Accounts who's dating your boss and your isopod will be like, "Hey, do you have time to look at an important report I've just drafted . . . *in my pants*?" through your gills.

Who needs a job anyway, right, Weeverfish?

The Master Deceiver

"No, you can't be something else when you grow up. You're not called a plumber bug, are you?"

IF YOU'RE GOING TO hunt the ultimate predators—spiders—you really have to know what you're doing. Along with bedbugs and aphids, assassin bugs fall into the "true bugs" category Hemiptera, a group based on the way mouthparts are arranged. In the assassin bug's case, this arrangement involves a needlelike proboscis: an elongated feeding tube separated into two barrels, one for injecting special anticoagulating saliva, and the other for siphoning blood and liquefied insides from its prey. But before it can siphon anything from said prey, the assassin bug has to figure out how to catch it.

In 2011, researchers from Macquarie University in Sydney examined the predatory behavior of *Stenolemus bituberus*, a local species of assassin bug known to feed exclusively on spiders and spider eggs. "Assassin bugs in general have some pretty bizarre behaviors, and we originally had the suggestion that *Stenolemus* assassin bugs have interesting predatory strategies from the field observations of a closely related species," says one of the team, biologist Anne Wignall.

Not all species in the assassin bug family are spider killers, or araneophages. Only those within the *Stenolemus* genus have demonstrated this behavior, according to Wignall. Their success lies in the fact that web-building spiders have very basic eyesight; their main sensory system is based on detecting vibrations. So whether the assassin bug decides to sneak up on a spider, or lure a spider toward it, it does not need to worry too much about being spotted, plus it can use the spider's reliance on reading vibrations against it.

First publishing in *Animal Behaviour,* the researchers reported that if an assassin bug decides to use what they called the stalking method, it will sneak up on a spider in its own web using irregular, bouncing movements while skillfully severing and stretching the silk threads between them, just like a *Portia* spider (see previous section, "The Spider-Eating Spider"). When the researchers pointed an electric fan at the web during this process, recreating the effect of strong winds, the assassin bugs were found to step more often and more continuously toward their prey, suggesting that they knew their movements were being masked by the vibrations caused by the "wind." So it would seem that together with the vibrations created by its cryptic movements, the assassin bug knows how to exploit periods of environmental disturbance, creating a "smokescreen" effect to cover its tracks.

Another study published that year by the team identified a second hunting technique: luring. When luring, the assassin bug will deliberately make short, low-frequency vibrations on the web to reveal its location and draw the spider toward it. The researchers watched as the assassin bugs cleverly plucked at the silk threads to emulate the twitching, panicked movements of ensnared prey for up to twenty minutes, tricking the spider into thinking it was about to get a meal. The results, published in *Proceedings of the Royal Society B,* revealed that the spiders' reactions to the assassin bugs' luring behavior practically mirrored their reactions to actual snared prey. The spiders would turn, pause, and approach the assassin bugs 65 percent of the time, and turn but not approach the assassin bugs in the remaining 35 percent of cases. The spiders would never approach the assassin bugs aggressively, which indicated that they had indeed been fooled. "Assassin bugs . . . tend to make low-frequency, irregular, low-amplitude vibrations. It sounds somewhat like prey in the web when struggling," says Wignall. "Picture a fly caught in the web, with its body in contact with the silk, rather than just the tarsi [or 'feet'] pulling, stretching, and tapping the silk. The vibrations assassin bugs generate are thought to mimic small or tired prey."

Wignall adds that when an assassin bug draws close enough to a spider, it will do something remarkable—it will begin gently tapping on the spider's leg with its antennae before slowly moving the taps along the abdomen to the cephalothorax, or head. While distracting the spider in this manner, the assassin bug will raise its head above the spider so it can stab down into it with those dagger-sharp mouthparts. "Whether luring or stalking, assassin bugs will always tap the spider at least a few times before stabbing it. This behavior is truly bizarre, as you would expect the spider at this stage to be alerted to the assassin bug's presence and either attack or run away," says Wignall. "We can see during hunts that the assassin bug actually makes contact with the spider's body with their antennae (and sometimes the spider will even move slightly in response to the assassin bug's touch). We still aren't sure what the function is, though we're working on it!"

Killer Cone Snail

GEOGRAPHIC CONE
(Conus geographus)

YOU'VE BEEN STUNG BY something in the ocean and now you're paralyzed. Nine hours later you're still so incapacitated that you can't stand up. And that's if you're very lucky. The worst part of this scenario is not that something in the ocean just almost killed you— it's that the something in the ocean that just almost killed you was a snail. Sure, it's one of the most dangerous snails in the world, but it's still just a snail and that's why your friends are laughing at you.

Armed with a cocktail of the most potent neurotoxins on Earth, the extremely rare geographic cone holds its own in an ocean full of weaponized fish, rays, and eels, having reportedly killed around thirty people so far in recorded history. There is no antivenom available and you have a 30 percent chance of being killed if stung. It may seem like a rather extreme weapon for a lowly snail to have, but when you move like a snail does, you need *something* to snare yourself a meal.

In 1932, British surgeon, pathologist, bacteriologist, and tropical shellfish expert Louis Hermitte reported that a patient of his had been stung by a geographic cone snail in the Seychelles Islands, where he was practicing at the time. This was the first such case reported from the Indian Ocean. After dissecting the snail, Hermitte discovered a radular tooth—a hollow harpoonlike structure—on the end of its extendable proboscis, a tubular appendage attached to the head that extends several times longer than the snail itself. A closer look led Hermitte to find that the snail also had a coiled venom duct to deliver venom to the radular tooth for injecting into unsuspecting fish. Researchers have suggested that in order to get their prey close enough to inject them, geographic cone snails release paralyzing chemicals into the surrounding water and then swallow them whole using a specialized billowy expanse of tissue. Once ensconced, the prey is stuck with a venomous harpoon so it can be devoured. This technique is so effective, it can bring down prey large enough to sustain the geographic cone for several days.

Of the 700 species of cone snail, the geographic cone is the most deadly. The venom used by cone snails is made up of active components called conopeptides—compounds consisting of 12–30 amino acids linked in a chain. According to Filipino-American chemist Baldomero Olivera, who has studied cone snail venom for over three decades, there are roughly 100–200 different conopeptides per species. This means that the composition of the venom differs between species, and even different individuals of the same species. Olivera says a shot of venom from a geographic cone is equivalent to eating a badly prepared piece of Japanese puffer fish while getting bitten by a cobra.

Olivera began his research by injecting the venom of the geographic cone into the abdomens of mice; they were immediately paralyzed each time. But in its original form, the geographic cone venom did not behave any differently from other known toxins, so Olivera lost interest. Then in 1975, a nineteen-year-old undergraduate student named Craig Clark from the University of Utah had the idea of taking isolated conopeptides from the venom and injecting them directly into the mice's central nervous systems. The results were stunning, says Olivera. The mice would display completely different symptoms depending on which conopeptide

Olivera and Clark injected, including shaking, sleeping, scratching, becoming sluggish, or convulsing. One of the peptides would even provoke different reactions depending on the age of the mouse receiving the venom. For example, a newborn mouse would immediately fall asleep, while a mature mouse would be worked into an uncontrollable frenzy. It was the bizarre effects of the conopeptides that prompted Olivera to consider that perhaps they had some kind of pharmaceutical potential.

Olivera found that each conopeptide worked by targeting a different type of molecule in the victim. He found that a great many of the molecules targeted were the types that control the flow of calcium, sodium, and potassium in and out of the cell. If you shut down these channels, as this venom does, messages between the brain and muscles cannot be delivered, which leads to shock and paralysis. Being able to home in on specific types of molecules made the cone snail toxins, or "conotoxins," ideal for medical research, because the ability to block calcium channels through the body can help patients with high blood pressure. What made conotoxins perfect for this is that they only seem to block the calcium channels in nerve cells, not those in the heart or other tissues, so side effects due to this treatment were limited.

Since Olivera's work, pharmaceutical companies have used conotoxins in treatments for an array of disorders such as epilepsy, cardiovascular disease, neurological disorders, and pain. In mid-2010, a team of Australian researchers reported that the venom of the marine cone snail (*Conus victoriae*), a species found in the waters of Western Australia and the Northern Territory, has potential as a painkilling medication. Based on their analysis of the marine cone snail's conotoxin, the team, led by chemist David Craik from the University of Queensland, synthesized an imitation conotoxin, added a few extra amino acids, and manufactured a painkilling pill that is many times more powerful than morphine. The team is hoping that this painkiller will completely revolutionize how scientists manage chronic and terminal pain in the future.

What a hero to little garden snails everywhere. Right now, dozens of snail fairy tales are being rewritten, because finally there's a snail that can do more than just move at the proverbial pace of itself.

So where snail-Rapunzel traditionally spent her entire life in the tower, reading, watching TV, making pesto, new Rapunzel would be rescued by a handsome geographic cone who launches his radular tooth up into her window like a grappling hook.

Where snail-Gretel traditionally shoves the snail-witch into the oven to save herself and snail-Hansel, new Hansel and Gretel will use their radular teeth to intimidate the snail-witch into building them a gingerbread mansion with a tennis court and Olympic-size pool.

New Snow White will be like, "You call this poison? Let me teach you a little something about poison, stepmother"; new Goldilocks will be like "All of these are pretty good. Three more bowls, slave bears!"; and new Three Little Pigs would be like, "Really, wolf? You're going to try to eat *us*? It's your funeral, dude."

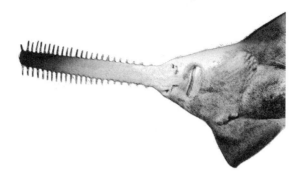

The Mystery of the Sawfish's Saw

SAWFISH
(Pristidae family)

LOOKING AT A SAWFISH, with its long, tooth-encrusted snout, it's hard to believe that the use of such a distinctive appendage has remained a mystery for so long. But catching one of these critically endangered animals in the act has been near impossible, so scientists have assumed that the sawfish, like every other jawed marine vertebrate with an elongated rostrum, or "beak," adheres to the rule that you use it to either sense or manipulate your prey. It's one or the other, scientists said, you can't have it both ways, and they had multiple examples of this occurring in other marine animals to back this up. The primitive, sad-looking paddlefish uses its extended, spatula-shaped rostrum to tune in to the electrical signals that give away the location of its prey, while members of the

billfish group, including swordfish, sailfish, and marlin, instead use
their slender, spearlike rostrums to physically stun their prey. And
sturgeons, which sport a relatively modest but electroreceptive rostrum, use theirs to rifle through the seabed, sucking up any prey
they locate.

The term "sawfish" describes seven species of ray that live in
marine, estuarine, or freshwater environments, four of which are
native to Australian waters. Their bodies are sharklike and they typically grow to be around 23 feet long. Along each side of the sawfish's rostrum, toothlike projections called rostral teeth poke out of
a great number of sockets, giving the animal a unique and intim-
idating appearance that sets it apart from other rays and the car-
tilaginous fish known as skates. While not considered a danger to
humans, anecdotal evidence of sawfish using their saws as a defense
mechanism includes an Australian man being chopped in half by
one, and dugongs who drifted too close being attacked in Indian
waters.

Oddly enough, until recently, only one—a smalltooth sawfish
(*Pristis pectinata*)—had been observed using its saw to actively
hunt prey, and this was in a controlled setting more than fifty years
ago. Because sawfish are so rare and their trade restricted to conservation purposes only, for years no one had properly studied
the function of the saw. It wasn't until vertebrate biologist Barbara
Wueringer from the University of Queensland published her PhD
thesis in 2010 that we began to get some understanding of how
they work, beyond being useful for raking through substrate on
the seafloor.

By examining four species of sawfish from northern Australia,
Wueringer discovered that the sawfish's saw is packed with thou-
sands of sensory organs called ampullary pores that can detect the

subtle electrical fields given off by moving organisms. The ampullary pores turned out to be more densely packed on the upper side of the saw, which suggests that sawfish are able to detect prey even in low-visibility waters using the whole three-dimensional space above it. This can cover a lot of ground if you're a green sawfish (*Pristis zijsron*), whose saw can grow up to 5 feet long. The result of Wueringer's initial study meant that sawfish were slotted into the group of jawed fish that used their rostrums for detecting prey, because at this stage, substantial evidence for hunting did not exist. So just like the enigmatic hagfish, says Wueringer, sawfish gained the reputation of being "sluggish bottom dwellers."

All of this changed when Wueringer got the chance to study a young, wild, longtooth sawfish (*Pristis microdon*) that had been accidentally caught by a fishing company and was on its way to an aquarium. Hidden cameras were installed in the sawfish's temporary tank to observe what it would do when fed chunks of tuna and mullet. When pieces of fish landed on the floor of the tank, the sawfish used its saw to pin them down and eat them, and Wueringer suggested that in the wild this mode of saw use would be particularly useful for manipulating spiny fish into a safe position for eating. When the fish pieces were floating through the tank water, the sawfish would slash back and forth at them, managing multiple swipes per second, to impale them on its rostrum teeth.

To confirm that this species was able not only to manipulate its prey, but also to detect it using its saw, Wueringer suspended electric dipoles—devices that mimic the electrical signals that surround moving prey—in the water and on the tank floor. Just as the different movements of the fish pieces, or "prey," prompted different aggressive responses from the sawfish, the different sources of the electrical fields brought about different detection responses from the sawfish. "Dipoles located on the substrate evoked predominately a biting response and sometimes 'wiggle' (a slight lateral movement of the head)," Wueringer reported in a 2012 issue of *Current Biology*. "Dipoles suspended in the water column evoked repositioning behaviors and 'saw in water' and 'wiggle', but never a biting response."

As part of the investigation, Wueringer compared the young sawfish's abilities to that of giant shovelnose rays (*Glaucostegus typus*) and eastern shovelnose rays (*Aptychotrema rostrata*), a pair of Australian species of ray with broad, triangular snouts that give their bodies a strange arrowhead look. In stark contrast to the agile and precise movements of the sawfish, the shovelnose rays were a mess. Wueringer reported that "[they] repeatedly bumped into and spiraled around dipoles suspended in the water column, in an uncoordinated fashion."

While sawfish have now been identified as the only jawed fish known to use their rostrum for both detecting and manipulating their prey, the appendage that gives them all their powers has also led to their devastating global decline. Their saws are just the right shape for getting accidentally caught in fishing gear, especially if they target the fish caught inside, but Wueringer hopes that research such as hers will lead to better conservation methods in the future.

A hushed silence descended on the room. Miss Scarlett checked her perfectly curled hair, twisting a strawberry blonde ringlet around a trembling finger tipped in carmine polish. Professor Plum tapped at his stalled pocket watch distractedly, muttering "Damn thing's never worked properly" to no one in particular. Mrs. Peacock shot him a glare from across the dining room table.

The door to the study swung open suddenly and Colonel Mustard stormed out, yanking a pipe from the breast pocket of his custom-made yellow tweed suit. A disheveled detective followed him out, stripped down to his undershirt and suspenders, his brow glowing with sweat. "Okay, Mrs. White, your turn."

Mrs. White was not coping well. The conditions in the mansion's kitchen were wreaking havoc on her health and the stress of the situation wasn't helping. She clutched her mother's brooch in her apron pocket for comfort as she entered the study. The detective closed the door behind her and told her to sit down.

"Look, Mrs. White, I'm going to make this quick," said the detective, standing over her with a knowing air. "I've ruled out every possible scenario, except one."

"And what would that be, Detective?" Mrs White asked, removing her wilted bonnet.

"It was you, Mrs. White, with the revolver, in the conservatory." The detective triumphantly snapped his notebook shut.

"What? Me? I *never*!"

"Save it, Mrs. White, it can't possibly have been anyone else."

"What are you talking about? The sawfish gardener was here the whole time! Why aren't you interrogating him?"

"I have my reasons, Mrs. White. We're going down to the station."

The detective put her in handcuffs to the astonishment of the remaining guests. The sawfish gardener watered the indoor palms in silence.

"I *knew* it!" Reverend Green declared, knocking his chair to the floor as he rose.

"Reverend! Some decorum, please!" exclaimed Mrs. Peacock.

"Show's over, everyone's free to leave," said the detective, dragging the raving cook out of the room.

"Fools! You've got it all wrong! It was the sawfish, look at him! Look at that saw! You're all mad! *Mad!*"

"Please, Mrs. White. The sawfish? Impossible! Everyone knows he only uses it for detection."

PART TWO

LOVERS AND
FIGHTERS

All-Female Lizard Tribe

WHIPTAIL LIZARD
(*Leiolepis ngovantrii*)

"Look, for the last time, we're not angry lesbians! We just considered all of the options and it makes more sense for us to reproduce on our own!"

"Ha! I told you she'd yell. You owe me fifty bucks."

IN 2010, A FATHER-SON team of American researchers announced their discovery that a popular Vietnamese lizard dish featured a species completely unknown to science. And these handsome lizards, with thick, grey skin decorated with tessellated brown and bright yellow spots along their backs, turned out to be particularly special, because they reproduce via parthenogenesis—a form of asexual cloning.

Named *Leiolepis ngovantrii*, after lead researcher and herpetologist Ngo Van Tri from La Sierra University in Riverside, California, these lizards belong to the 1 percent of lizards and 0.1 percent of vertebrates that have done away with the need for sexual reproduction. Earlier in 2010, molecular biologist Peter Baumann from the Stowers Institute for Medical Research in Kansas City, Missouri, who was working with a different type of asexual lizard, figured out exactly how it's done.

The whiptail lizard family from North America and Mexico contains some fifty species, one-third of which are all female. In the 1960s, professor of medical science William B. Neaves from the Stowers Institute ran a genetic analysis of lizards from the *Leiolepis* genus in the whiptail family. Looking at the results, he suggested that all-female whiptail species came about through a hybrid cross between a female of one sexually reproducing species and a male of another. Prior to this discovery, it was assumed that the males of these species were super-elusive—no one had imagined that they simply did not exist. "We now know that at least in vertebrates, interspecific hybridization has given rise to most, if not all, unisexual species," says Baumann.

What wasn't clear from these initial studies is how the hybrid she-lizards were able to maintain the diverse mix of genes from their parent species, which allowed them to survive and produce healthy offspring for several thousand generations over an extensive geographic area. Species with clonal offspring lacking any genetic material from a male parent often have very low genetic diversity, which can result in poor adaptability and vulnerability to disease because these genetic weaknesses have no chance of being overridden by new genetic material from a mate. Many hybrids, such as the mule, turn out to be sterile. But somehow whiptails have managed to overcome this fundamental problem in asexual reproduction to produce healthy offspring at a rate identical to that of sexually reproducing species. "In our experience, the reproductive success is very high and indistinguishable from sexually reproducing lizards," says Baumann. "This is quite different from some arthropods where the hatch rate of parthenogenetically produced eggs is only 10 percent."

Baumann and Neaves developed thirty microsatellite markers—specific pieces of repeating DNA that are used in genetic studies to identify parentage and kinship—and found that there was considerable variability in these pieces of DNA across species in the *Aspidoscelis* genus of the whiptail family. This variability appears to allow mutations to occur, which ensures the robustness of the asexual lizards. And how they achieve this variability through cloning is nothing short of genius.

In sexual reproduction, each parent contributes half of its chromosomes to their offspring. The random combination of the parents' chromosomes results in the offspring having a complete and unique set of chromosomes. Reporting in a 2010 issue of *Nature*, Baumann and Neaves described how the process of meiosis (where the number of chromosomes are halved in order to create an animal's egg or sperm cells) in asexual whiptail reproduction begins with cells containing 92 chromosomes—twice the number of their sexual peers—resulting in eggs containing 46 chromosomes. So while eggs from sexual species end up with just 23 chromosomes, whiptails have figured out a way to pass on an adequate amount of genetic material despite the fact that their eggs are never fertilized. "We are now trying to understand the molecular events that result in premeiotic doubling of chromosomes," says Baumann. "One can speculate that there is something in the genetic makeup of these animals that predisposes them to activate parthenogenesis upon hybridization. We would like to know what that is."

It is still unclear what triggers the reproductive process in the whiptails, but there has been some speculation that a behavior called pseudocopulation, which involves two females mounting each other to stimulate egg production, is required. But Baumann remains skeptical of this, pointing out, "When we keep a unisexual lizard by herself from the day she hatches out of the egg, she will produce just as many or more offspring than lizards housed in groups."

At this stage, it is unclear whether the all-female whiptails will some day in the future become a sexually reproducing species once more through another round of hybridization, resulting this time in sexually reproducing offspring. But if they do remain partheno-genetic, they might have the success of other parthenogenetic species such as the bdelloid rotifers. These near-microscopic aquatic animals, or "evolutionary scandals," as Baumann puts it, have sur-vived as unisexuals for many millions of years and have even radi-ated into species groups without having sex.

And considering how costly sexual reproduction is in terms of resources, will other parthenogenetic species arise in the future? Males use up resources such as food, shelter, and water without contributing much to the next generation. A unisexual species comprised of only females will grow much faster assuming that equal numbers of offspring are produced, because each individual in that species has the capacity to produce offspring on her own. "Graham Bell called this 'the queen of questions in evolutionary biology,'" says Baumann. "What is the advantage of sex that is large enough and acts on a short enough timescale to outweigh the two-fold cost of sex [more resource use for less offspring]? Clearly 99.9 percent of all species reproduce sexually, but we still don't under-stand why that is so."

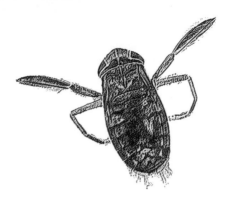

The Loudest Penis
on Earth

AT JUST 0.08 INCHES long, the lesser water boatman is the loudest animal on Earth relative to body size. And perhaps even more impressive is the fact that this tiny insect makes its noises using not its mouth or legs or wings—it makes them using its penis.

In mid-2011, engineering expert James Windmill from the Centre for Ultrasonic Engineering at the University of Strathclyde in Scotland reported in *PLoS ONE* that the lesser water boatman (*Micronecta scholtzi*) can produce sounds at a level of 99.2 decibels, which is equivalent to sitting in the front row of a theatre and listening to a loud orchestra play. It achieves this through a process known as stridulation, which describes the rubbing together of two body parts to create a song that can travel over large distances. One of the most commonly heard products of stridulation is performed by grasshoppers, who scrape their hind legs against their adjacent forewing to produce their characteristic chirping sound. Crickets and katydids stridulate in the same way. The water boatman, on the other hand, rubs his penis against his abdomen in an effort to court females.

The lesser water boatman is a freshwater insect, found in ponds all over Europe—the more stagnant, the better. One of four species in the *Micronecta* genus, the lesser water boatman can be identified by its genitals and distinctive head pattern. From August 2009 to September 2010, Windmill and his colleagues collected a number of lesser water boatmen from a river in Paris and put them in plastic water tanks fitted with hydrophones—microphones specifically designed to record sounds underwater. Because water boatmen are only active in groups, the researchers put five in each tank, and then recorded the calls of thirteen males.

On average, the songs reached 78.9 decibels, which is equivalent to the sound of a freight train hurtling past 49 feet away. Fortunately for the people living around this river in Paris, or anywhere near a lesser water boatman, most of the sound doesn't make it to human ears, says Windmill. According to his research, while 99 percent of sound is lost as it is transferred from water to air, the lesser water boatman's song is so loud that if you're walking along the bank, you can actually hear it singing from the riverbed.

Lesser water boatmen produce their songs to get females to notice them, and the loudness may be the product of what's known as runaway or Fisherian sexual selection. A song produced at the loudest possible level might scramble the quieter songs emitted by competitors when the males call to the females in a chorus.

Common sense dictates that natural selection would counterbalance runaway selection, as the loudest songs are the deadest giveaways for predators, but the researchers suggest that the lesser water boatmen don't have predators that track them by sound, which is what has led to their boisterous songs.

The male produces the song by rubbing its pars stridens—an organ also used to grasp onto the female during copulation—against a particular abdominal ridge. What makes the volume of the song so impressive is that this ridge is only about 0.002 inches long, approximately equal to the width of a human hair. Plus, unlike all other species of stridulating organisms, the water boatman does not seem to possess any body parts that act to amplify the sound. So just how such a tiny insect can use its even tinier penis to produce such an impressive song remains a mystery.

Oh man, Lesser Water Boatman, how annoying would you be literally every time you talk to a female? I know being really loud is what you have to do for courting purposes, but just be aware that every time you take a girl on a date, it ruins everyone else's night.

Say you're in a restaurant on a first date with some girl you met on the Internet, and you're all, "SO NICE TO FINALLY MEET YOU IN PERSON."

The waitress will glower at you and half the patrons are going to leave while your date buries her face in her menu because she's so mortified. She'll say yes to a second date out of equal parts kindheartedness and cowardice, so you'll take her to the movies. You'll be like, "JEEZ *THAT'S* A SMALL COKE? WHAT'S THE LARGE SIZE, A CRUISE LINER? LOLOLOL." And then the movie will start and you'll be like "I THOUGHT HE WAS THE BAD GUY, BUT NOW I THINK MAYBE HE'S GOOD?" and "UH OH, ALL THAT COKE HAS REALLY MADE ME WANT TO PEE."

Sorry, Lesser Water Boatman, but unless you can figure out how to lower your courting voice, you're going to have to settle for a romantic career of picking up girls in a nightclub, where you're literally the only male any of them can actually hear.

Battle of the Genitals

"It's hopeless! Every time we add some length or a new barb to our penises, the females respond with another dead end or another coil in their oviducts! We're running out of ideas!"

"Why don't we just stop forcing ourselves on them, then?"

"Hahahahaha. Good one."

BEING MALE DOESN'T NECESSARILY mean you need to have a penis. Most birds, amphibians, reptiles, and monotremes don't have one. Instead, they have a cloaca, which is a multipurpose opening on the rear for the intestinal, reproductive, and urinary tracts. If you're a male with a cloaca, it acts as a vent for sperm, plus, rather unromantically, urine and excrement.

About 3 percent of birds have opted to keep the penis-vagina method of reproduction, but things are not any better for them either. Thirteen years ago, the existence of avian phalluses was brought to the attention of behavioral ecologist Patricia Brennan from the University of Massachusetts, when she saw birds called tinamous mating in Costa Rica. While biologists have known for decades that some birds have penises, it seemed that Brennan was the first to ask, and investigate, the question, "Why do ducks have penises?"

"My first interest was in studying why so few birds have maintained a penis while most birds have lost it," says Brennan. "I began looking at ducks because they are the most common bird group where all species have a penis. There was virtually nothing known about bird genitalia when I first started doing my research, and the variation among species in the morphology (the form and structure) is so striking, that it seemed a great system to explore in detail."

The male duck, or drake, penis, is very different from the male mammal penis. Each species equips a different variation, with lengths ranging from 0.5 inches to over 16 inches, some adorned with feathers, spines, or grooves. They can begin as tiny organs, a matter of hundredths of an inch, when the duck is growing, but can often end up long and twisted, like a slender tentacle extending from the cloaca wall. They are kept folded inside a phallic sac until provoked, when they will be forced out, quick as a flash, by an immune system fluid called lymph (rather than blood). The Argentine blue-bill duck (*Oxyura vittata*) from South America boasts the longest penis relative to body size of any animal in the world, one famous specimen packing a 17-inch-long penis inside its 8-inch-long body. The drake's penis grows at the beginning of the reproductive season and shrinks right down at the end, possibly because that's the easiest way to keep such an enormous organ clean for a lifetime.

But what of the female ducks' genitals, if they must somehow accommodate such a serpentine monstrosity? As Brennan told British science writer Carl Zimmer for a 2007 *New York Times* article, "You need a garage to park the car." By 2005, Brennan had discovered something that, shockingly, no other biologist had ever thought to look for—female duck vaginas, or oviducts, are more incredible, complex, and labyrinthine than ever imagined. Publishing that year in *PLoS ONE,* Brennan described the oviducts of sixteen species of waterfowl to find that while each species had a different oviduct form, ranging from short, narrow, and muscular cavities to extremely long, complex, and counterclockwise-spinning tunnels, each one matched the complexity of the corresponding male. So in species such as the long-tailed duck (*Clangula hyemalis*), Brennan found that both the females and the males had equally elaborate genitalia.

Another thing the males and females of both of these species had in common was a high level of forced copulations. This suggests that the females have been developing highly complex oviducts to prevent being successfully fertilized by forceful males' sperm. "Female ducks cannot behaviorally avoid unwanted copulations, and often times they are subdued by multiple males who can copulate in quick succession," says Brennan. "Females can then only use what we call copulatory or postcopulatory strategies to regain control of the reproductive decisions, in this case, which male will gain paternity of her offspring." She adds that typically females will try to use more subtle strategies than this, such as simply ejecting sperm from unwanted males, but this technique doesn't always work because the males can use their long penises to deposit sperm further inside the female's oviduct than is possible to be ejected. "Since these structures only are found in female ducks in species where forced copulations occur, it is likely that they evolved in response to these unwanted copulations," says Brennan.

According to paternity data for a number of species of duck, forced copulations can be very common—40–50 percent of all observed copulations, according to Brennan. But only 2–5 percent of a female duck's offspring turn out to be the results of forced copulation. While a female's mate will try to defend his paternity by mating with his female immediately after a forced copulation has taken place, it's primarily thanks to the females' natural chastity belt that these forced copulations are not very successful. "If the female's own mate could defend his paternity fully, there would be no need for the females to evolve the convoluted vaginas, but the fact that they do suggests that they are primarily responsible for preventing successful fertilization of eggs by unwanted males," says Brennan.

Not that the males are necessarily the losers of this ongoing evolutionary arms war—they have certain tricks up their sleeves, too. In late 2009, Brennan published a study in *Proceedings of the National Academy of Sciences* on Muscovy ducks (*Cairina moschata*), which are a large species native to Central and South America and Mexico. The males are around 34 inches long while the females are about 25 inches long, and they both have bare, bright red skin surrounding their eyes and beaks. Brennan wanted to study the mechanics of the Muscovy duck's penis, so she had four 0.4-inch-diameter glass tubes created: one in a simple, straight shape; one in a counterclockwise corkscrew that matched the male's penis spiral; one in a clockwise corkscrew that ran in the opposite direction to the male's penis; and one with a 135-degree bend, which resembles the first dead-end kink in the female's oviduct.

Because male ducks only have an erection directly into the female's oviduct, as opposed to becoming erect some time before copulation, Brennan needed to very quickly intercept the male with each of the four tubes as he mounted a female to see how easily his penis could unfurl in the different shapes. She found that the male's penis easily made it through both the straight tube and the tube that mirrored the shape of its coil, the explosive erection filling the tube in less than half a second. But the clockwise corkscrew-shaped tube and the bent tube posed a much bigger challenge. Brennan also found that when males were mating with real females, if a female was happy to mate with a male, and the copulation wasn't forced, she would maneuver herself in a way that helped the male's penis find its way through her twisted oviduct. This suggests that female ducks still have the upper hand in the decision of who will father their offspring, because they can control to what extent their oviducts act as a natural sperm barrier.

The Impossible Mates

"Guys, this is so ridiculous. Haven't any of you heard of tequila?"

IN JUST THREE MOUNTAIN ranges in central China, 1600 giant pandas are eking out an existence in the only environment in the world that can sustain their very particular lifestyle and diet. A nearby earthquake is all it would take to wipe out an enormous chunk of what habitat these pandas have left, which is exactly what happened in Sichuan in 2008. A magnitude 8.0 earthquake, which released as much energy as the detonation of 6 million tons of TNT, destroyed more than 23 percent of the wild pandas' habitat in this province in southwest China, which researchers from the Research Center for Eco-Environmental Sciences at the Chinese Academy of Sciences in Beijing estimate to have affected 60 percent of the entire wild giant panda population.

Adding to their environmental woes are the giant pandas' notoriously complicated reproductive needs. Female giant panda reproduction has been extensively studied, and it's well known that they are sexually receptive at just one moment per year, between February and May. And the female panda's estrus, which is the state of sexual excitement that comes immediately before ovulation, lasts just 24–72 hours within this three-month window. This means that the female giant panda devotes less than 1 percent of its entire life to sexual activity.

So we know how female giant pandas contribute to breeding difficulties with captive pairs, but until recently, very few studies had been carried out on the males. In April 2012, an international research team led by veterinarians Copper Aitken-Palmer of the Smithsonian Conservation Biology Institute at the American National Zoo in Washington and Rong Hou of the Chengdu Research Base of Giant Panda Breeding in Sichuan, China, published the results of a study of eight captive male pandas—the first time this many have been studied at once. Over three years, the researchers observed a range of factors in the male pandas including sperm concentration, testes size, reproductive behavior, and the levels of androgen, which are hormones that determine the development and maintenance of male features. They found that, like the females, the males exhibit seasonal waves of reproductive activity, with all of the above increasing during the October to January period, in preparation for the females' period of reproductive activity, and well into the breeding season between February and March.

According to the study, which was published in *Biology of Reproduction*, the males' testes volume and sperm concentration were at their peak from March 22 to April 15—directly coinciding with the females' peak breeding activity. After this period, the males' reproductive behaviors began declining from April 16 to May 31, returning to their lowest point in the year from June through September.

Despite the fact that the male pandas' bodies spend an entire year preparing for the sliver of time that the females actually feel like having sex, captive breeders still find it extremely difficult to successfully mate a pair, with some 60 percent of male pandas in zoos or enclosed sanctuaries showing no sexual desire whatsoever.

In 2002, researchers at the Wolong Nature Reserve in Sichuan tried giving their male pandas Viagra, but to no avail. In 2007, zookeepers at Thailand's Chiang Mai Zoo tried something a little different with their giant panda pair: Chuang Chuang, a six-year-old male, and Lin Hui, a five-year-old female. First, the couple was separated in the hopes that they would begin lusting after each other, and then Chuang Chuang was put on a diet so he wouldn't crush Lin Hui when—if—he attempted to mount her. Alone in his cage, Chuang Chuang was made to watch "panda porn," which is video footage of other panda pairs mating, to sexually arouse him. The same technique was used in China in early 2006 to produce thirty-one cubs in a ten-month period, twenty-eight of which survived. Unfortunately for the Thai zookeepers, even after two weeks' training, which involved making Chuang Chuang watch the porn video for fifteen minutes a day, he did not respond by being sexually aroused.

Because of their complicated reproductive needs, breeding giant pandas is becoming increasingly difficult, and the remaining population is dwindling so rapidly that a number of scientists consider it too late to save the species. In late 2011, environmental economist Dr. Murray Rudd of the University of York questioned 583 scientists via e-mail about whether we should consider setting up what's known as a conservation triage. Where wildlife is concerned, a conservation triage means we should focus our resources on threatened species that we have a good chance of saving, and give up on the more difficult or "expensive" threatened species such as pandas and tigers. Rudd reported that almost 60 percent of the scientists he polled agreed or strongly agreed that "criteria for triage decisions should be established." It's a sobering thought that in just a few generations' time, there might not be any giant pandas left.

Don't Trust Them with Your Offspring

WHEN IT COMES TO seahorses, it's the males who bear the responsibility of pregnancy. The same goes for their relatives the pipefish, whose males are equipped with a specialized external brood pouch into which the females will deposit eggs during copulation. But a recent examination of pipefish male pregnancy and mate selection has found that this process is nothing to coo over.

Observing the reproductive behavior of twenty-two captive male gulf pipefish (*Syngnathus scovelli*), a small-mouthed, pencil-shaped species with a relatively poor swimming technique, biologists Kimberly Paczolt and Adam Jones from Texas A&M University discovered just how much control the males have over their prospective progeny. By pairing the males with either large or small females, the researchers found that the males wasted no time in mating with larger, more attractive females, but were significantly less eager when paired with smaller females. They also found that the eggs deposited by larger females had a much higher rate of survival to the point of birth, with the males selectively aborting those from a less attractive partner by either withholding vital nutrients, or absorbing (in other words, cannibalizing) the embryos.

By also looking at successive pregnancies in male pipefish, Jones and Paczolt were able to make sense of these rather callous tendencies. Not only do broods from smaller females have a low survival rate to begin with, but if a male first mates with an attractive female and bears a large brood, he's unlikely to want to invest more resources into a subsequent pregnancy, particularly from a less attractive partner. Instead of nurturing these offspring, his specially evolved brood pouch allows him to retain or absorb the nutrients to ready himself for the possibility of meeting a more attractive mate.

"The bottom line seems to be, if the male likes the mum, the kids are treated better," says Paczolt. "Why this occurs, we don't fully understand. But our findings are quite specific about this relationship between the male pipefish and its mate. If the male prefers the female, he treats their mutual offspring better."

That the male pipefish are actively trying to control the quality of their offspring during pregnancy is evidence of postcopulatory sexual selection, which follows the initial competition for mates by way of combat and elaborate courtship displays. But postmating sexual selection, such as things that happen within a female's reproductive tract or the dogged competition of sperm, remains something of a mystery, just like male pregnancy. "The whole phenomenon of male pregnancy is full of conflict and far more complex than we had previously realized," says Paczolt.

Well, gulf pipefish boys, you might think this is all pretty great, being able to pick and choose (and cannibalize) your own progeny with nary a qualm in the world. But the thing is, those ugly pipefish girls you mated with in the past—they're not just going to disappear. The ocean might be big, but it's not that big, and you know what they say: "Mate with one ugly pipefish that time you had nine vodkas, three gins, and no dinner, and you'll end up with six months of whiny text messages and a lifetime of really awkward encounters whenever you try and go back to that particular bar because they have $4 spirits till 1 A.M."

So you'll decide to risk it and go to this bar one night, all like, "Five tequila sunrises please. Oh. Hi . . ."

And that unattractive pipefish girl you once mated with will be like, "So how are the offspring?"

"Huh?"

"You know, the offspring. *Our* offspring?"

"Oh. Umm. Hmm . . ."

"You ate them all, didn't you?"

"Well, technically I absorbed . . . Shit."

And now you're wearing five tequila sunrises, gulf pipefish boys. But it won't end there, because everyone will know that you mated with her, especially her really short and ugly friends, and they'll look at her and then at you and then back at her and figure they've got a shot.

So you'll be at a completely different bar, trying to chat up some cute pipefish girl, like, "I aborted a brood hoping to meet someone so . . . long. How many millimeters are you, anyway? Wait right there, I'm going to buy you so many drinks."

But you'll only get halfway to the bar before a bunch of short and ugly ladies will crowd around you all, "Hey can I buy you a drink?"

"No."

"You want my number? I might be only 4 inches long, but I sure know how to use each one . . ."

And meanwhile the cute pipefish girl will think you're not into her, so you'll either have to go home alone or settle for one of the short and ugly pipefish girls.

And you thought having a brood pouch would be a riot, gulf pipefish boys.

Your Mother Wants
You to Eat Her

LIFE AS A JUVENILE black-lace weaver spider is far from easy. As part of a group known as subsocial spiders, which describes a species that on occasion displays co-operative behavior, a black-lace spider will hatch with some 60–130 siblings and remain on a communal web with its mother. The spiderlings will live off a second batch of eggs laid by their mother, which sustains them for a week or so before they are old enough to lead the traditional solitary lifestyle of a spider.

But before the black-lace spiderlings can go out on their own, their mother will encourage them to devour her body, giving herself up as their final family meal. Research has shown that compared to spiderlings that are denied this meal, spiderlings that eat their mother are more likely to survive after they leave the nest.

This is not the only cooperative behavior displayed by young black-lace weaver spiders, which can be found in North America and Europe. In mid-2010, biologist Kil Won Kim from the University of Incheon of the Republic of Korea reported the results of the first study examining the synchronization movements in nonsocial or subsocial spiders in *Insectes Sociaux*. She discovered that once the spiderlings have eaten their mother and taken over her web, if they feel threatened, they will group together and contract their bodies in unison to make the web pulse. This behavior, which emerges just one day after the act of matriphagy (eating one's mother), is typically triggered by the approach of intruding insects, mites, or worms, leading Kim to suggest that this functions as an antipredatory strategy.

An individual spiderling senses this potential threat, contracting its body, and approximately 60 percent of the other spiderlings will follow suit, contracting and relaxing their bodies to create an eerie pull-and-release effect on the web that is never performed while the mother is still alive. According to Kim, the function of this pulsing may be to fool an approaching predator into thinking that a much larger animal is nearby, convincing it to flee.

The black-lace juveniles use this technique for seven to nine days after matriphagy, by which time they appear to grow out of it, focusing their collective efforts on hunting prey up to twenty times their size instead. The spiders will continue living in a large sibling group for three to four weeks after the death of their mother and then leave the web to live alone, now old enough to fend and hunt for themselves.

Spiderling. Just . . . ugh. I mean, how does this work exactly? You're all sitting around the dinner table like, "Hey Mum, look how many eggs I can fit in my mouth," and "Do you think Justin Bieber likes spiderlings?" when suddenly she's like, "So . . . who wants to start on my abdomen?"

And you'll be all, "WTF, Mum!"

"Watch your language and eat my abdomen."

"But Mum . . . Does this mean we have to pay our own school fees now?"

You'll reluctantly slink off your chairs and edge toward her, telling each other that you'll probably be grounded either way, but she's much less likely to enforce it if you eat her. Someone will sheepishly point out that she actually tastes all right, and before you know it, you'll be collectively digesting your mum while watching something with Selena Gomez in it.

But then what? I'm sorry to break the news, spiderlings, but huddling together on your web, contracting nervously in unison, muttering, "Oh my god, oh my god, we're all gonna die," isn't going to solve your problems once the predators find out what's really going on. You need a more sophisticated plan. And that's where I come in. But first you'll need:

- A precocious attitude
- An empty house, preferably in the initial stages of being renovated
- Paint tins
- Rope
- Bricks
- A blowtorch
- Staple guns
- Live electrical wires lying in a pool of—

What? Too complicated? Oh for Christ's sake, spiderlings, haven't you ever seen *Home Alone*?

Fruit Bat Fellatio

"Mr. Greater Short-Nosed Fruit Bat, I'm very happy to inform you that you're a finalist for our community achievement award. Have you got anything to add to your nomination that might give you an edge over the other finalists?"

"I'm one of the only animals in the world to frequently engage in oral sex?"

"Good lord. That's hardly relevant, Mr. Greater Short-Nosed Fruit Bat."

"Yeah, I know. But any excuse to say it out loud."

You wouldn't know it by looking at them, but the greater short-nosed fruit bat is one of the most sexually liberated members of the animal kingdom. This fist-sized, burnt-caramel–colored species has been declared one of the only animals in the world to engage in oral sex—and possibly the only animal in the world, besides humans, to engage in *frequent* oral sex.

In 2007, researchers from the East China Normal University and Institute of Zoology at the Chinese Academy of Sciences published a study in *Biology of Reproduction* reporting that fruit bats are one of the few mammal species that experience menstrual cycles. Two years later, a team of entomologists lead by Min Tan from the Guangdong Entomological Institute in China discovered something similarly unusual about the mating behavior of greater short-nosed bats (*Cynopterus sphinx*).

Preferring to keep the company of not one, but a harem, of females, a male greater short-nosed fruit bat will construct elaborate tents from stems and leaves, holding them in place with saliva. Taking 30–50 days to complete, the tents provide shelter for the male and the multiple breeding partners he recruits to defend their food stores and produce offspring.

Tan's team set up a group of thirty male and female bats in cages filled with large Chinese fan palms, perfect for tent making, and observed their behavior over a month as various harems were established. They found that while grooming themselves or tending to their palm roost, a male would be approached by a female, who stretches out her wings to reveal their leathery girth. The bats then lick and sniff one another, before the male climbs onto the female's back using his thumbs to adjust himself into a face-to-back mating posture. With the male keeping a firm grip on the female by holding her wings tightly in place with his thumbs and the scruff of her neck in his mouth, the pair will mate.

The researchers were surprised to find that during fourteen of the twenty copulations, the females would frequently lower their heads to lick the shaft or the base of the male's penis, which appeared to encourage penile stimulation, stiffening, and erection. "There was a strong correlation between the total length of time that the female licked the male's penis and the duration of copulation. Therefore the longer the female licked the penis of her mate, the longer they copulated for," the team reported. They found that for every one second of fellatio there were approximately six extra seconds of copulation. Regarding the six instances that licking behavior was not apparent, the researchers suggested that the female was mating under duress, because she would evade the male for several seconds.

According to the researchers, this behavior holds several adaptive benefits for the greater short-nosed fruit bat species. Tan offers four hypotheses to explain its penchant for genital licking. The first and second relate to lubrication and penile stimulation, both of which serve to prolong copulation and assist the successful transmission of sperm to the female. The third hypothesis relates to how mate choice in bats can be influenced by chemical signals. Tan's final hypothesis relates to the possible prevention of sexually transmitted diseases (STDs) between the sexes. It has been known for some time that bat saliva boasts antibacterial, antifungal, antichlamydial, and antiviral properties, which scientists have in the past tried to incorporate into human medications. Right now, researchers including Robert L. Medcalf from Monash University in Perth are working on a stroke medication derived from the anti-blood-clotting saliva from vampire bats, aptly named Draculin.

While Tan and his colleagues say that their observations are the first to show regular fellatio in animals other than humans, fellatio is not unheard of in other animal species. In separate studies published in 1995 and 2004 by Dutch primatologist Frans de Waal and Italian primatologist and sociobiologist Elisabetta Palagi, it was found that oral sex was a type of "play behavior" performed by young male and female bonobos, an endangered species of great ape. "In general, many animals may lick genitals before and after copulation, for example, the male of [the] ring-tailed lemur, *Lemur catta*, often licks the genitals of the female in order to judge whether she is in estrous (ready to mate), and after copulation, he also licks his penis," Tan and colleagues wrote in *PLoS ONE*. Similarly, said the researchers, both male and female Livingstone's fruit bats (*Pteropus livingstonii*) also licked the genitals of their partners during heterosexual interactions, but it's unclear whether they actually perform fellatio during copulation. So until further research says otherwise, greater short-nosed fruit bats remain almost peerless in their fondness for fellatio.

It's Time to Become Gonads

DEEP-SEA ANGLERFISH
(*Ceratiidae family*)

BEING AN ANGLERFISH MALE would be the absolute worst. As proud as most males in the animal kingdom tend to be of their genitals, the idea of actually *becoming* genitals by fusing yourself to your mate is a bit much. Unless you're an anglerfish male, in which case it's just something that has to be done. Some people have to be garbage collectors, others have to be genitals.

The bizarre reproductive habits of deep-sea anglerfish were first described in 1922 by Icelandic fisheries biologist Bjarni Saemundsson, who discovered a large female Krôyer's deep-sea anglerfish (*Ceratias holboelli*) with two smaller fish attached to her stomach by their snouts. What Saemundsson didn't realize was that these tiny fish weren't young offspring taking nutrients from their mother, but sexually mature males. "I can form no idea of how, or when, the larvae, or young, become attached to the mother; I cannot believe that the male fastens the egg to the female. This remains a puzzle for some future researcher to solve," he wrote in the journal *Videnskabelige Meddelelser fra Dansk Naturhistorisk Forening*.

Three years later, British ichthyologist, ecology, and evolution expert Charles Tate Regan found a similar situation. This time a single small fish was fused to a female, and Tate recognized it not as a mother-offspring relationship, but a parasitic male-female relationship, reporting in *Proceedings of the Royal Society B*:

> [The male fish is] merely an appendage of the female, and entirely
> dependent on her for nutrition . . . so perfect and complete is the
> union of husband and wife that one may almost be sure that their
> genital glands ripen simultaneously, and it is perhaps not too fan-
> ciful to think that the female may possibly be able to control the
> seminal discharge of the male and to ensure that it takes place at
> the right time for fertilization of her eggs.

Anglerfish belong to an order Lophiiformes, which is a highly diverse group of fish boasting an array of shapes, including elongated, spherical, and flattened bodies, living 985 feet below the surface. There are around 200 species of anglerfish spread around the world's oceans. Anglerfish in the family Ceratiidae, also known as sea devils, live at depths of 0.6–2.5 miles in the bathypelagic zone where not a speck of sunlight exists. They are famous for the reproductive process that sees free-swimming adolescent males attach themselves to a female and morph into a living, parasitic set of gonads.

Members of the Ceratiidae family are generally top heavy with relatively large heads and jaws filled with many tiny teeth set into an extreme underbite position. The females of each species are adorned with a bioluminescent lure that extends from their foreheads in myriad shapes, sizes, and lengths. Characteristic of the Ceratioidea is their extreme sexual dimorphism, which describes a genetically determined difference between males and females of the same species expressed by their morphology, behavior, or ornamentation. In birds, sexual dimorphism is the difference between the stunningly beautiful male peacock and its drab female counterpart, and in the Ceratioidea's case, this means large females and significantly dwarfed males. So dwarfed are the deep-sea angler-fish males, measuring an average of just 0.2–0.4 inches in their free-swimming, adolescent stage, that they are one of the world's smallest vertebrates. In the most extreme cases, such as the Krôyer's deep-sea angler- fish, the females can be up to sixty times larger than the males, more than 3 feet in length, and half a million times heavier.

While Ceratioidea males lack the female's bioluminescent luring apparatus, which is formed by the foremost three spines on her first dorsal, or back, fin, they do have large, well-developed eyes and gigantic nostrils in their adolescence. Researchers have suggested that these are used for homing in on a special hormone emitted by the females. When a male finds a female, it will start to metamorphose, its eyes and nostrils degenerating while its teeth are replaced by large pincers. These are used to grip on to a prospective mate, which begins the fusing process of the male's mouth to the female's body. Some species see just one male attaching itself to a single female, while in other species a female can host up to eight dependent males. Although it may seem like an unnecessarily complicated process to get the males and females to reproduce, researchers suggest that it is the only way, because without fusing with the females the males will never reach sexual maturity. And likewise, the females will never become gravid, meaning capable of carrying eggs internally, unless they have a male attached. According to American systematist and evolutionary biologist Theodore Wells Pietsch III, one of the world's experts on anglerfish, "That sexual maturity is determined not by size or age in these fishes, but by parasitic sexual association, may well be unique among animals."

Publishing a study in *Ichthyological Research* in 2005, Pietsch said that in some species of Ceratioidea, the fusing of flesh involves the combination of circulatory systems, which means the males depend entirely on the females for their continued survival, "while the host female becomes a kind of self-fertilizing hermaphrodite." Pietsch adds that the males increase:

> considerably in size once fused, their volume becoming much greater than free-living males of the same species, and being otherwise completely unable to acquire nutrients on their own, the males are considered to be parasites. They apparently remain alive and reproductively functional so long as the female lives, participating in repeated spawning events.

Pietsch, who is currently the curator of fishes at the Burke Museum of Natural History and Culture at the University of Washington, has been studying anglerfish for over twenty years. In early 2012, he went to bat for them when a group of scientists, led by Louisiana State University graduate student Eric Rittmeyer, declared a newly discovered species of frog the world's tiniest vertebrate.

Publishing in *PLoS ONE*, Rittmeyer and his team described *Paedophryne amauensis*, a copper and black frog from New Guinea averaging just 0.3 inches in length. Pietsch challenged the new frog's inclusion in the *Guinness Book of Records* promptly after the paper had been published, arguing that the free-swimming adolescent male of an anglerfish he described in his 2005 paper stretches just 0.24 inches, making it 11 percent smaller than *Paedophryne amauensis*. But due to the fact that females of the same species are up to six times bigger than the frog, Rittmeyer's team was not convinced. For now, it looks as though the title of World's Smallest Vertebrate is subject to opinion.

Journal Notes: Deep-Sea Anglerfish
June 3
I never knew my father. Mother told me as soon as I was old enough to understand that he was gone before I was born. My friends all say the same about their fathers, but it doesn't make it hurt any less. That he didn't want to stick around to see what I'd look like, what I'd act like, which college I'd end up going to. So that's why I'm going to learn everything I can about him, discover what clues he left behind so that I might come to understand who I am and who I will become. Ate lunch, got indigestion like always. Note to self: eat slower.

June 5
Questioned Mother while she was making dinner. Got mostly cagey responses but she put chilies in our meal, which she never does, so suspect chili is some kind of clue. Suspect Mother is trying to tell me something. Called the Chili Palace, man on phone didn't seem to want to talk

about anything but chili dogs. Suspect he and Mother are in cahoots. Watched *Downton Abbey*. Hated it.

June 6

Googled Dad. Discovered that he was a tailor and had a shop in town that's now a comic book store that I can't go into anymore because I'm in love with the girl who works there. Found photo of my English teacher wearing one of Dad's Prince of Wales suits while attending a production of *Uncle Vanya: The Musical* on *Sea Morning Herald* society site. Googled *Uncle Vanya: The Musical*, universally panned, but there's a good chance Chekhov liked chili, so ordered a dog from the Chili Palace. Indigestion.

June 9

Just realized something. Got the Chili Palace receipt out of my bin: $4.44. Which corresponds to all Ds in the alphabet. Ds for "Dad." I'm really onto something here. Showed Mother to see if her reaction would give anything away and she said not to use her credit card again.

June 10

Learned about the whole morphing-into-genitals thing in sex ed class today. Contemplating becoming a ~~warlock~~ whatever the male version of a nun is.

Sexy Monkeys Bathe in Urine

SO, MONKEYS COAT THEMSELVES in urine to become more attractive to the opposite sex. Not exactly surprising, seeing these are the same animals that love a good spot of public masturbation.

Of the New World group of monkeys, which includes squirrel monkeys, marmosets, howler monkeys, capuchins, and tamarins, a number of species are known to wash themselves in their own urine by urinating into their hands before vigorously rubbing them all over their feet and fur. Many hypotheses have been proposed to explain the behavior, such as thermoregulation—the urine cools them down—communication between rivals, communication during sexual encounters, and recognition of other individuals of the same species via their scent, but for years no one was able to come up with conclusive evidence one way or another.

Primatologist Kimberley Phillips from Trinity University in San Antonio, Texas, decided to peer into the minds of these curious primates to find out what information the signals in their brains could provide. "I was at the zoo one afternoon, observing monkeys, and just thinking about their behavior," says Phillips. "It was one of those 'aha' moments, especially when I realized we could use brain imaging to assist in solving this puzzle."

Capuchin monkeys belong to a genus of over twenty species ranging over tropical and subtropical South and Central America, including Peru, Bolivia, and Brazil. Depending on the species, capuchins can be black, brown, burnt caramel, or cream, with their nude pink faces peering out of their soft, dense fur. They are relatively small, never growing over 11 pounds, and agile, built to spend their days hopping between trees, using their long, slender tails for grasping and balance. When the females are sexually receptive, they will actively solicit a male, and previous studies had shown that when this happens, the selected male will step up his urine washing. "Every capuchin I've seen—in the wild and in captivity—has engaged in this behavior at some point," says Phillips.

She tested the reactions of a group of captive-born female tufted capuchins (*Sapajus apella*) to urine collected from both adult and juvenile males. Using magnetic resonance imaging (MRI) scans, she was able to detect the activation of regions in the brain associated with smell and sexual behavior in the females far more when they sniffed the adult males' urine than when they sniffed the juvenile males' urine. Because the sexually mature males provoked the greater response in the females, Phillips reported in a 2011 issue of the *American Journal of Primatology* that she had found conclusive evidence that at least one of the functions of urine washing was sexual communication. "I wasn't surprised that urine washing served a role in sexual communication, as this type of pheromonal communication occurs in a variety of other species; but I was a bit surprised that the neuroimaging results turned out so nicely," she says. "But we did not discount other functions of this behavior. It is likely that there are other communicative and other functions as well."

The Capuchin Monkey's Guide to Getting Laid

Hi guys, a lot of you have been asking me for some dating advice because I dated a Kardashian that one time, so I've decided to post a little dating guide here so all you losers actually have a shot.

Lunch Date

Lunch dates are pretty noncommittal and depending on the rate of service at whatever establishment you choose, you can usually get it over pretty quickly if you decide halfway through you're not that interested in her after all. When you're getting ready to go, make sure you choose a fairly casual outfit; you can get away with being too casually dressed if you're witty or pretending to be a scruffy shipping heir, but you can never come back from accidentally trying too hard with your clothes. Grab your keys, wallet, and phone, pee on yourself, head out the door.

The same pretty much goes for dinner dates, except add flowers, plus you can get away with applying a little bit more pee.

Hot New Girl's First Day in Your Office

Make friends with the IT guy who can see her desk from his and get him to tell you when she's heading toward the kitchen for tea or something. Pee on yourself. Meet her in the kitchen and tell her about how you prefer Lady Grey because then she'll think you have sophisticated taste buds.

In the Club

Shots, pee on yourself, shots, repeat.

Next week: my guide to picking the right kind of suit for every occasion.

Secret Boys' Club

MEET THE LITTLE FROG that gives a new meaning to telephone.

While most frogs have their eardrums on their body surface, the concave-eared torrent frog has ultrathin eardrums recessed inside its ears. This extremely rare species from the Huangshan Hot Springs west of Shanghai in China is one of only two frog species known to possess this kind of ear—the other being the wonderfully named hole-in-the-head frog from Borneo.

Being recessed, the ultrathin eardrum, which in the males is about one thirtieth the thickness of an average frog's, is protected, and the shortened path between the eardrum and the ear allows it to detect very high-frequency sounds. While average frogs are restricted to hearing frequencies below 12 kilohertz, concave-eared torrent frogs can produce a chirp at a phenomenal 128 kilohertz. This ultrasonic frequency is more than six times higher than humans can hear.

Only a select few animals in the world are known to belong to the "ultrasonic club" and the researchers who discovered the ability suggest that it was developed in response to the extremely loud babbling of the streams and waterfalls around which they live. "Nature has a way of evolving mechanisms to facilitate communication in very adverse situations," says the lead author of the study published in *Nature* in 2006, Albert Feng from the University of Illinois, who discovered the frogs' ability. "One of the ways is to shift the frequencies beyond the spectrum of the background noise. Mammals such as bats, whales, and dolphins do this, and use ultrasound for their sonar system and communication. Frogs were never taken into consideration for being able to do this."

In their study, Feng and colleagues discovered that during the reproductive season, the male concave-eared torrent frogs were adding ultrasonic calls to their regular calls, broadcasting their message over several frequencies at once. The researchers recorded the calls and played the audible and ultrasonic ranges to eight males in captivity. At the time, it was assumed that, like with most frog species, the female concave-eared torrent frogs were not physically capable of calling. The researchers found that six of the males responded to calls played back in both the audible and ultrasonic range, only one responded exclusively to the ultrasonic call, and only one responded exclusively to the audible call, suggesting that calls at the audible and ultrasonic frequencies could have different meanings.

At first it was thought that only the male concave-eared torrent frog males could emit, and respond to, ultrasonic calls, making territorial calls to one another and letting the females know they are around. In most species of frogs, the females don't call, firstly because they don't have the vocal equipment required, and secondly because the males do it so they don't have to.

Because concave-eared torrent frogs are nocturnal and capable of jumping thirty times their body length they make difficult test subjects in the wild, which means it wasn't until Feng and colleagues got the females in a laboratory setting that they realized how special these females are. In 2008, they discovered that the female concave-eared torrent frogs, like the males, can emit high-pitched birdlike chirps spanning the audible and ultrasonic frequencies. Publishing in *Nature*, the team reported that when the females were looking for males in captivity, they would emit an ultrasonic call, to which males would respond by leaping toward the call with 99 percent accuracy. "This is just unheard of in the frog kingdom," says Feng.

Just how the female picks a male in the wild is as yet unclear. Is she calling a particular male, or is she signaling her whereabouts so multiple males can find her and compete? "We have a lot of work to do to figure out whether she directs the signal to one male or whether she lets a bunch of males come and compete, or whether there is any kind of dueling session during which she then decides: 'Okay, you're my guy. Hop on my back and I'll take you to the creek!'" says Feng.

Things got even more complicated in 2011, when a study led by the coauthor of the 2006 and 2008 studies revealed that the female concave-eared torrent frogs might not actually be able to hear sounds emitted at the ultrasonic frequency. The females have thicker eardrums than the males, and no ear canals, which suggest that it's possible they're not as well equipped to hear at superhigh frequencies, despite being able to make ultrasonic calls.

Jun-Xian Shen from the Institute of Biophysics at the Chinese Academy of Sciences took females from the wild and first played them the males' calls at the audible frequency and then the calls at the ultrasonic frequency in a dark room. Each time the audible calls were being played, the females responded by turning and jumping frequently toward the source, and sometimes they even called back. But when the ultrasonic calls were played the females neither moved toward the source, nor responded vocally.

To test whether or not the females were simply ignoring the calls, the team measured their auditory brain responses as they listened to the males' calls. When lower frequency calls at the auditory frequency were played, a peak of activity in the females' midbrains could be seen, indicating that they were picking up the sounds. But nothing over 16 kilohertz provoked any kind of brain activity, which shows that, as the structure of their ears suggests, the females simply cannot hear at very high frequencies.

So why is this? The researchers suggested that unlike the males, who need to be out looking for females and making themselves known above the sounds of the waterfalls around them, the females spend a lot of their time in rocky cracks, trees, or muddy caves, where the sounds around them are muffled. Perhaps the females simply don't need to hear sounds at such a high frequency. According to Shen, who published the findings in *Nature Communications*, this is the first demonstrated amphibian, bird, or mammal species in which the males have the capacity to hear at the ultrasonic frequency but the females likely do not.

Seriously, female concave-eared torrent frogs, get a load of these jerks. They have their own language now? Why can't they just e-mail each other about . . . whatever it is boys talk about? Do they really need an entire secret language so they can make comments about the concave-eared torrent frog equivalent of boobs at any possible opportunity?

I guess it would be pretty handy at the bar. They can literally decide who they're going to go home with right in front of your faces, like, "Okay you can take the hotter one and I'll take the less hot one, but I get to use your basketball season tickets for the whole of January." "Deal, but you're buying drinks." "Deal." And you'll be like, "What are you guys talking about?" and they'll be like, "Stocks?"

And then one of them will say something to the other one—you can tell, female concave-eared torrent frogs, because their mouths are moving—and they'll both start snickering to each other really obnoxiously and you'll be like, "What are you guys LOLing about?" and they'll be like, "Stocks?"

But whatever, female concave-eared torrent frogs, let them have their own secret language, you be the bigger man in the scenario. They can talk about whatever the concave-eared torrent frog equivalent of boobs is in front of your faces and they can LOL about how your best friend clearly wants to do all of them (I'm right there rolling my eyes with you, female concave-eared torrent frogs), but you'll always be the only ones who actually *have* the concave-eared torrent frog equivalent of boobs, and there's nothing the least bit funny about LOLing about something you just LOL'd your way out of seeing.

A Love Affair with Beer Gone Wrong

AUSTRALIAN JEWEL BEETLE
(*Julodimorpha bakewelli*)

SOMETIMES IT IS POSSIBLE to love beer just a little too much. The Australian jewel beetle is a glossy, golden-brown beetle around 1.6 inches long, found all over Australia in arid and semi-arid areas. It belongs to the Buprestidae family of jewel beetles, so-called because of the iridescent coloring running through the 15,000-odd species, including shimmering greens, purples, blues, and bright yellows.

In late 2011, the Harvard University–based *Annals of Improbable Research* blog awarded its annual Ig Nobel Prizes, the aim of which is to "honour achievements that first make people laugh, and then make them think." Last year's biology category was won by two entomologists, Darryl Gwynne from the University of Toronto at Mississauga in Canada and David Rentz from the

Australian national science agency, the CSIRO, for their research into the strange sexual habits of the Australian jewel beetle more than twenty years ago.

In September 1981, Gwynne and Rentz stumbled on something remarkable in the Dongara area of Western Australia, 218 miles north-northwest of Perth. "It was pure serendipity and a happy coincidence because I study these differences in behavior. We did not set out to study the beetles. David Rentz and I . . . happened to stumble across the beetles one sunny morning on our field trip," says Gwynne.

The pair observed male Australian jewel beetles flying 3–7 feet above the ground at the Dongara site, scouting for the large, flightless females, when two of them landed and started trying to mate with a 0.8-pint beer bottle, widely known as a "stubbie." "We have recently observed this to be quite a common occurrence in the Dongara area of Western Australia," they reported in the *Journal of the Australian Entomological Society* in 1983. This behavior was first observed by Australian zoologist Athol M. Douglas from the Western Australian Museum, who published photographs of a male Australian jewel beetle mating with a stubbie, as well as another being attacked by a handful of ants during the act, in 1980.

Surveying the area, the entomologists found two more males mating with their own stubbies, and just one stubbie without a beetle was located. They conducted a brief experiment at the site, which involved placing four stubbies on the ground in an open area to see if they would attract the beetles. Within half an hour, two of the bottles had attracted males, and beyond that time frame, four more were observed to mount the arranged stubbies.

The behavior was put down to the beer bottles' basic visual similarities to the large Australian jewel beetle. The shiny brown color of the glass resembles that of the beetles' coloring, plus the dimpled glass at the base of the bottle and the tiny bumps on the beetles' elytra, or hardened forewings, both reflect light in the same way. The contents of the bottle held no attraction for the males; in fact, stubbies with beer left in them were left entirely alone, and when bottles of different shades were left out for the male beetles by the entomologists, they were also ignored. "It looks like it is visual cues," says Gwynne. "We washed out bottles to rule out ethanol and the color and patterning of the bottles resembles the brown wing covers of the beetles."

Just how these males could make such an unfortunate mistake in identifying females of their own species is less clear, but Gwynne suggests it has to do with the difference between how the males and females of the Australian jewel beetle species choose their mates. "Males typically compete, take risks, and occasionally make mating errors. Females are typically choosy and get mated in a nonrisky way," he says, and adds:

> The lion's share [of investment in offspring] typically comes from the female because—even in species with no parental care—the female invests so much in the egg, compared to the male invest-ment in the tiny sperm. As a consequence, producing offspring for males is cheap so they are always playing the mating game.

As ridiculous as this all sounds, this behavior can have serious effects on the male Australian jewel beetles. Gwynne and Rentz described how once on the bottles, the males would not stop trying to copulate with them until they were physically displaced. In the wild, this means they could unwittingly starve or exhaust them-selves to death—according to Gwynne, they observed some males falling off the bottles with heat exhaustion—and render themselves completely vulnerable to predators such as ants. Ants are known to attack and eat the lovelorn males alive, as Douglas had observed twelve months earlier. "In one of the observations, a male, at the side of the bottle, was being attacked by a number of ants (*Iridomyrmex discors*), which were biting at the soft portions of his everted genitalia. A dead male, covered with ants was located about an inch away from this same bottle," Gwynne and Rentz reported in their 1983 paper. "Improperly disposed of beer bottles not only present a physical and 'visual' hazard in the environment," they concluded, "but also could potentially cause great interference with the mating system of a beetle species."

Okay, sure, Australian jewel beetle males, those stubbies look "similar" to your females. Because they're both long and brown. Or you're all just superdrunk and covering for each other. Which is fine, you're allowed to all go to the pub together and talk about sports and beer till 4 A.M. You're even allowed to get so loaded that you try to fuck a stubbie every once in a while. It's cool, we've all been there. But when it gets to the point where you're actually getting *killed* over it, Australian jewel beetle males, it's probably a good time to ease up on the beers. Just a bit.

Or you can just keep going as you are and get eaten alive by other insects and when your children ask why you didn't come home last night, your wife—yes, your *wife*, Australian jewel beetle males, you do actually have one—will have to tell them you fucked yourself to death and now they can never have new shoes. And the kids will be like, "Well at least he died *getting it on*," and your wife will be like, "Nope, he was fucking a stubbie." And the last thing your children will ever say about you, Australian jewel beetle males, is "Holy shit, Dad was a total pervert."

Won't Rat You Out
for Chocolate

RAT
(*Rattus*)

"I'm here to save you! You're *free!*"
"Are you insane? This is a change room, get the hell out of here!"

RATS TEND TO GET quite a bad rap because of their disease-harboring abilities, but in some aspects, we're really not that different from rats. Nature is rife with animals that display prosocial behavior, which essentially means looking out for your peers. Even insects such as bees and ants display this kind of behavior, but unlike humans and other primates, they don't "share" in the distress or pain of someone else: They don't display empathy. Until very recently, it was not known if nonprimate mammals were similarly motivated by empathy, but it turns out that not only do rats look out for their fellow rat, they will give up *chocolate*, of all things, to do it.

A small team of scientists led by psychology postgraduate student Inbal Ben-Ami Bartal from the University of Chicago stumbled on just how empathetic rats are when testing the effects of stress on food sharing amongst them. "Like many scientific discoveries, this one was accidental, or rather serendipitous," says Bartal, adding:

I was testing the restrainer that we were planning to use inside one of the home cages. When I trapped the rat, I noticed the free rats started circling the restrainer frantically, and seemed distressed, to my untrained eye. I repeated the experiment with a different cage the next day, and realized that I might be seeing something overarching. Then we thought about allowing the free rat to release the trapped rat.

Bartal and her colleagues designed and set up experiments in which two rats that normally share a cage were moved into a test arena. One rat was held captive in a small restrainer device that could only be nudged open from the outside, while the other rat was left free to run around the arena, able to see and hear the distress of its trapped cagemate. The researchers observed that the free rat acted far more agitated when it was in the presence of a trapped rat compared with being in the arena with an empty restrainer, exhibiting what's known as "emotional contagion," a phenomenon that occurs in animals with the capacity for empathy—they can share in the fear, distress, or pain experienced by their peers.

The rats didn't just "feel" the distress of their trapped cagemates, they also actively set about improving their situation by figuring out how to open the restrainer door and free them, taking multiple tries before eventually becoming quite proficient at it. To make sure the rats were acting purely in the interests of their cagemate, the researchers tested their behavior in another setup, whereby opening the restrainer door, the free rat would release the trapped rat into another compartment. This meant the reward of social interaction had been discounted—and sure enough, the free rat continued to release its cagemate. The experiment had shown that the rat had no other reason to free its cagemate other than to put an end to its distress. "We were not surprised by the rats' behavior, since multiple studies have demonstrated emotional contagion in rodents. But we were surprised at how robust this behavior was, and how persistently free rats would continue to circle the restrainer—they would continue this behavior for hours," says Bartal.

To test just how robust the rats' need to stop the suffering of their cagemates was, the researchers gave the free rats a choice—release your companion from the restrainer, or focus your attention on securing a delicious treat for yourself instead. They placed free rats in an arena with a trapped cagemate as well as another restrainer filled with a pile of chocolate chips to see which restrainer the rat would concentrate on. They found that the free rat was equally likely to open the restrainer to free its cagemate before focusing on the chocolate restrainer, which meant that putting an end to the distress of a fellow rat was equally as rewarding as hoeing into a pile of chocolate chips. In cases where the free rat released its cagemate before working on the chocolate restrainer, 52 percent of the time it would share the chocolate with its cagemate, the researchers reported in *Science*.

But not all rats displayed such "honorable" behavior. About 25 percent of the rats tested failed to free their trapped cagemate. Bartal says while it's unclear exactly why this occurred, it could be due to the different personalities in the rats: Some were too stressed out, others couldn't figure out how to open the restrainer, and others were just plain mean. "Some are 'scaredy rats' who are too overwhelmed with personal distress to be able to successfully assist the trapped cagemate (opening the door is hard and the rats need to move around a lot and keep trying in order to figure it out). Some rats are unable to figure out the door opening, and there is the occasional bully who appears to be uninterested in opening the door and even attacked the trapped rat once he gets out. Now we want to see what distinguishes those populations out, biologically," says Bartal. Another idea she plans to test is what happens when the free rat and trapped rat are strangers, or even competitors. Does empathy in rats have its limits?

PART THREE

ANCIENT
CREATURES

The Largest Feathered Animal Ever

"So I don't look 'fierce' with all these feathers. Who cares? I'm fabulous!"

TYRANNOSAURUS REX HAD A gigantic feathered cousin, according to newly discovered fossil evidence, which proves that feathered dinosaurs were bigger than we could have ever imagined.

The Tyrannosauroidea was one of the longest-living subgroups of theropods, which were bipedal (walking on two rear legs), mostly carnivorous dinosaurs. According to the fossil record, their existence spanned from the Middle Jurassic, which lasted from 176 to 161 million years ago, to the Late Cretaceous, around 65 million years ago. At this stage, they had achieved apex predator status across the Northern Hemisphere and some species were seriously outgrowing their ancestors, reaching over 2200 pounds in weight and up to 33 feet in length.

In mid-2012, the discovery of one such dinosaur was reported by a team of scientists led by paleontologist Xing Xu from the Chinese Academy of Sciences in Beijing, who has discovered some thirty new species of dinosaurs so far. They unearthed the new tyrannosauroid from the Lower Cretaceous level of the Yixian Formation, which is an extremely fossil-rich formation in Jinzhou, Liaoning, in the northeast of China, which spans about five million years within the early Cretaceous period. The Yixian Formation has produced a wealth of surprisingly well-preserved fossils of everything from feathered dinosaurs and the most ancient bird species to fish, spiders, flowering plants, pterosaurs, and mammals. But this new dinosaur was particularly special.

Named *Yutyrannus huali*, which means "beautiful feathered tyrant" in a combination of Latin and Mandarin, the dinosaur was pieced together from three 125-million-year-old near-complete skeletons, namely one adult and two juveniles found alongside fossilized pieces of sauropod—the remnants of a hunt, perhaps. The researchers, publishing in *Nature*, described *Y. huali* as having weighed a hefty 3098 pounds and stretched 30 feet long, with relatively long forearms for a tyrannosauroid. But most incredibly, each specimen showed signs of having been coated in a down of 6-inch-long filamentous feathers which, rather than being like the flat, rigid feathers of a modern crow or seagull, would have been similar to the thick plumage sported by modern emus and cassowaries. This makes *Y. huali* the largest feathered animal ever known, around 35–40 times the size of the previous record holder, *Beipaiosaurus*, a Chinese dinosaur with a disproportionately compact head, a stout, stocky body, humungous claws exploding from its forearms, and clumps of feathers around its neck, rump, and tail. "The discovery of *Y. huali* provides solid evidence for the existence of gigantic feathered dinosaurs and, more significantly, of a gigantic species with an extensive feathery covering," the researchers concluded.

Due to the apparent structure of *Y. huali*'s feathers, Xu and his team have suggested that their function was less to do with flight and more to do with insulation, as it is with today's flightless birds sporting similar filamentous fuzz. But exactly why this occurred is pretty puzzling, seeing as very large animals, such as elephants and rhinoceroses, retain heat very easily and find it difficult to keep their body temperatures down. This is why they need thick hides instead of dense fur coats. The researchers considered what the environmental conditions would have been for *Y. huali* and noted that this area in China would have been considerably cooler 125 million years ago, suggesting that, like the woolly mammoth and the American bison, it lived in a cold enough environment to warrant a fuzzy winter coat, in spite of its large size. "[The] presence of long feathers in the gigantic *Y. huali* could represent an adaptation to an unusually cold environment," they wrote. "*Y. huali* lived during a period that has been interpreted as considerably colder than the rest of the Cretaceous (a mean annual air temperature of about 10 degrees Celsius (50°F) in western Liaoning, in contrast with about 18 degrees Celsius (64°F) at a similar latitude in the Late Cretaceous)." This is of course speculation, and because the plumage had only been partly preserved on each of the three specimens, the researchers were careful to point out the possibility that, like *Beipaiosaurus*, *Y. huali*'s plumage was restricted to certain parts of its body. In this case there's a chance their feathers performed more of a display function than a warming one.

Of course, it's time to discuss the elephant in the room, which is the question of whether this discovery can tell us any more about whether or not *T. rex* was similarly fuzzy. While we don't have any direct evidence of it yet, and *T. rex* did live in a climate that was much warmer than *Y. huali*'s stomping ground, the possibility can't be ruled out. "*Yutyrannus* dramatically increases the size range of dinosaurs for which we have definite evidence of feathers," says Xu. "It's possible that feathers were much more widespread, at least among the meat-eating dinosaurs, than most scientists would have guessed even a few years ago."

A Venomous Dinosaur?

IN 2009, A CONTROVERSIAL paper suggested that a group of small, birdlike therapods might have been venomous. The study, published in *Proceedings of the National Academy of Sciences* and led by paleontologist Enpu Gong from the Chinese Academy of Sciences, centered on an unusual half-inch-long tooth from the top front row of the mouth of a *Sinornithosaurus*—a genus of feathered dinosaur that lived more than 120 million years ago. Not only did the researchers find this tooth to be very long and fanglike, but they found a thin, distinct groove running right through it from root to tip, which Gong suggested could have functioned as a channel for venom to pass from the animal's skull into the flesh of its prey. A hollow pocket in the side of the *Sinornithosaurus*' face, evidenced by the shape of its fossilized skull, was identified as a possible venom gland, and a pitted canal running between it and the base of the teeth could have acted as a venom-collecting duct.

Modern venomous snake species can be separated into two groups, front fanged and rear fanged. Front-fanged snakes are the most common group—all Australian venomous snake species, including the red-bellied black snake, are front fanged—their hollow, syringelike teeth are designed to inject a very potent venom into the flesh of prey. Rear-fanged snakes such as the vine snake are far rarer, their fangs sitting further back in their mouths on the upper jaw. Running along the back of each tooth is a groove through which a mild form of venom drips, its purpose related to digestion rather than defense or killing.

Citing the teeth of rear-fanged snakes as morphologically similar to the unusually long *Sinornithosaurus* maxillary teeth, Gong suggested that this predatory raptor would have hunted mainly small birds and mammals, using its fangs to "grab and hold" its prey, penetrate the layer of feathers or fur and deliver a 0.2-inch-deep bite. Like rear-fanged snakes, the dinosaur might have had to chew on its prey to dispense enough venom into its body to induce a shock response. "The poison of *Sinornithosaurus* may have been similar in properties to rear-fanged snakes and helodermid (bearded) lizards in that it did not kill the envenomated animal quickly but rather placed it into a rapid state of shock," he said.

But Gong's claim is not without its critics. Tom Holtz, a paleontologist who specializes in carnivorous dinosaurs at the University of Maryland, responded by saying the unusual length of the fangs could have been caused by regular-sized teeth slipping out of their sockets after the animal had died. He also suggested that the grooves could simply be the depressions found in most theropod teeth, only more pronounced in this particular specimen due to wear and tear. For many years, paleontologists have believed that the function of these depressions relates to how bayonet blades function, the groove helping to relieve surface tension once the tooth has penetrated a surface, which ensures a less painful extraction. Holtz added that many dinosaurs have a small cavity in their jawbones, but these have typically been interpreted as air sacs required for cooling, not pockets for venom glands.

In 2010, a group of paleontologists from Argentina released a paper in *Paläontologische Zeitschrift* agreeing with Holtz's criticism of Gong's venom theory: "We fail to recognize unambiguous evidence supporting the presence of a venom delivery system in *Sinornithosaurus.*"

Gong and his team responded by publishing a paper in the same issue of the journal, arguing that recent research led by venom expert Bryan Fry from the Australian Venom Research Unit has indicated that venom glands in lepidosaurs (a subclass of scaled lizards which includes the common iguana) are far more common than thought, so it would be a mistake to assume that archosaurs (a group including extinct non-avian dinosaurs, crocodilians, pterosaurs and modern birds) with grooved teeth had no venomous taxon, or group, in their ancestry, and were not venomous themselves. It's an issue that remains unsolved, but no dinosaur has so far ever been conclusively proven as having been venomous. This means the onus is on Gong and his team to come back with some unambiguous proof for their claim.

Arguments aside, *Sinornithosaurus,* say you did actually have this venomous bite. I'd imagine it'd be the kind of thing you could easily get carried away with, like an out-of-control James Bond. Say, for example, you're playing *Sonic Racing* at *Dromaeosaurus laevifrons*'s house all, like, "Hey, remember when games didn't go so fucking fast that you could actually see where you're going? Christ, we're old," when *D. laevifrons* will tell you, "I'm going to make a sandwich. If you cheat when I'm gone I'll know."

"But it's almost midnight . . ."

"Just because *you* can't have carbs before bedtime . . ."

"Dick."

So you'll unpause and move your Shadow forward a bit because he just implied that you're fat, but you'll underestimate just how anal *D. laevifrons* is and the moment he gets back, he'll be like, "Oh my god, you totally cheated."

"No I didn't."

"Yeah, right. Hey, what are you doing . . . Hey! Heeey!"

"Oh. Sorry. My mistake."

"That was my leg. Jesus! That really hurts. Wait, you're leaving? Right now?"

And before he can point out that if you bring a bottle of wine to someone's house, you're not really supposed to take it home with you just because you drank his wine instead, he'll go into shock, and you'll grab the leftover quiche, too.

But the only lesson you'll learn from this whole experience, *Sinornithosaurus*, is how easy it is to get out of a shitty situation by, you know, injecting your friends with venom. Like, you'll be at your girlfriend's house and she'll try on this hideous new dress she just bought and she'll be like, "Does this make me look fat?" and it will, *Sinornithosaurus*, so you'll be like, "Erm, hey look behind you!"

"What? . . . Ow!"

Your boss will ask you what the hell kind of report that was you left on his desk (no kind, *Sinornithosaurus*, it was terrible), so you'll bite him and take the rest of the day off. You won't have any cash to buy an ice cream so you'll bite the shopkeeper. And while you might think this is all pretty great, remember, *Sinornithosaurus*, this kind of behavior isn't without its consequences. Which means you'll be at some party with your new girlfriend and somehow your ex will turn up all, "I don't want to make a scene, but injecting me with poison was a really dick move, even for you." And then your current girlfriend will be pissed because she didn't even know you had an ex, let alone one you injected with poison and left for dead, and they'll end up being best friends just to spite you. Plus your boss will almost definitely fire you when you show up for work on Monday and every shopkeeper in town will close his doors in your face, and your best friend isn't speaking to you anymore, because he's dead. Hardly seems worth it now, does it, *Sinornithosaurus*?

What's That on Your Face?

"I want to break up."

"What? Why? We've been getting along so great!"

"Yeah, I know, I'm just not ready for a relationship, and I'm just . . . confused about things. You know?"

"You looked in my medicine cabinet, didn't you?"

"No. Okay, *yes*. You're disgusting."

"I'm not the one who ate an entire tube of Pringles by myself last night."

"I'm sorry, I couldn't hear you over all the noise your face lesions are making—"

"What lesions?"

"—through that cheap concealer you're trying to hide them with."

"Goddamn."

UNUSUAL LESIONS AND PUNCTURE marks found on the skulls of *Tyrannosaurus rex* and other tyrannosaurid species have revealed that a common avian infection might have plagued these ancient predators. And infighting appears to have been the factor that spread it.

In a 2009 paper published in *Palaios,* a team of scientists from Northern Illinois University and the Burpee Museum of Natural History described the results of their examination of "Jane," a 23-feet-long *T. rex* skeleton found in the Hell Creek Formation in Montana in 2011. With a slightly asymmetrical snout and four partially healed oblong lesions along the left side of her skull, it's been suggested that Jane shows evidence of aggression amongst juvenile tyrannosaurs as they compete for dominance, territory, or resources. The team compared the positioning and orientation of the lesions along Jane's nasal and upper jaw regions to the jaw shape of the only fossilized vertebrates found in the Hell Creek Formation that were large enough to inflict such wounds—other theropods and crocodilians. They found that the size, shape, and spacing of the fossilized juvenile theropod teeth corresponded convincingly to the positioning of Jane's lesions, unlike those of the crocodilians.

Evidence of face biting is not uncommon in the tyrannosaurid fossil record, but this is the first indication that this kind of behavior was not just restricted to fully matured adults. As Jane's age has been estimated to be around twelve years—two years prior to the age of sexual maturity for the *T. rex*—the researchers were able to rule out the possibility that this was strictly part of courtship-related behavior. They also found indications of partial healing through bone repair, which suggests that though this face biting was not typically fatal, it could cause a slight warping of the muzzle as it remodeled itself. "Jane has what we call a boxer's nose," says Joe Peterson, geologist from Northern Illinois University and lead author of the study. "Her snout bends slightly to the left. It was probably broken and healed back crooked."

That same year, a study published in *PLoS ONE* led by paleontologist Ewan Wolff from the University of Wisconsin described a parasitic infection that causes severe erosion of the jawbone and ulceration of the mouth and esophagus, ultimately leading to death by starvation. Of the sixty-one tyrannosaurid specimens Wolff examined, 15 percent of them had the telltale signs of this infection—several smooth-edged pits in the lower jawbone. While these were quite distinct from the rougher-edged bite marks found in Jane's skull, in many of the specimens examined, both kinds of lesions were present, suggesting that the infection could have been transmitted through face biting in much the same way as the face cancer now threatening to drive Tasmanian devils to extinction.

Wolff also discovered that the lesions caused by infection were remarkably similar to those found in the beaks of modern birds such as turkeys, chickens, and pigeons that have been infected by a parasite called *Trichomonas gallinae*. Modern birds can pass on trichomoniasis by simply touching each other on the beak, which can lead to severe ulceration of the upper digestive system and ultimately starvation. This suggests that there could have been a shared affliction between modern birds and extinct tyrannosaurid species, which is yet further evidence of how closely the two groups are related.

King of the Rabbits

NURALAGUS REX

"Your Majesty, the enemy troops are lined up at the shoreline. What would you have us do?"

"Sit on them."

"Your Majesty?"

"Sit on them. Sit. On. Them. What are you, deaf? Because the only person who should be deaf in this castle is me. Do you see how small my ears are?"

"Begging your pardon, Your Majesty, but I'm not sure any of us are big enough to sit on our enemies and make a difference . . ."

"I have *one* other strategy for situations such as these but I'm reluctant to tell it to you because if you fuck it up we'll all be doomed."

"Your Majesty?"

"I learned this tactic when I was just a boy, and my father, King Rabbit VI, had to defend his kingdom from some kind of enemy force, I can't remember what. He said to me, 'Son, never fuck this strategy up, because if you do, we'll all be doomed.' So the enemies were lined up at the gates, launching lit arrows over the walls. The women and children were screaming and the entire kingdom thought everything was lost, but then my father . . ."

"Your Majesty?"

" . . . My father . . ."

"Yes . . . ?"

"Nope, it's gone. But that makes sense, because I'm the only person in this castle with a head too small to fit a reasonably sized brain inside, so why the hell aren't you people doing my thinking for me? As King of Minorca by virtue of being the most giant animal here, I command you to go out there and sit on our enemies. How do you think I became king in the first place? Wits? And tell the kitchen I'm hungry again."

WHAT A DIFFERENCE A few million years can make. We may be used to the relatively manageable bundles of fur and breeding that are modern rabbits, but no one was prepared for their ancestors to be hulking great stubby-eared monsters that can't jump. In 2011, a team of paleontologists led by Josep Quintana from the Institut Català de Paleontologia in Barcelona announced the discovery of a new species of extinct rabbit called *Nuralagus rex*—literally, "King of the Rabbits."

During the Late Neogene period, which ended about 2.5 million years ago, *N. rex* lived on Minorca, a small Spanish island belonging to the Balearic archipelago in the western Mediterranean Sea. So strange was *N. rex* that it took years after a complete skeleton of one was extracted from slabs of red limestone for researchers to identify it as a massive, lumbering rabbit. "When I found the first bone, I was nineteen years old. I was not aware what this bone represented. I thought it was a bone of the giant Minorcan turtle!" says Quintana.

Publishing in the *Journal of Vertebrate Paleontology,* the researchers described *N. rex* as having weighed around 27 pounds—six times the size of a regular European rabbit (*Oryctolagus cuniculus*). And unlike the long, flexible spine that modern rabbits have, *N. rex* had a compact, rigid backbone and short legs, which meant it couldn't hop, or even run. More likely it was slow and hunchbacked, and spent its days burrowing for roots and lazing about on the Minorcan beach. It also had a compact head with beady eyes, short ears, and a small brain so, unlike modern rabbits with their keen eyesight, acute hearing, and incredible agility, the King of the Rabbits showed no sign of needing to spot and escape from predators.

According to the researchers, *N. rex* represented one of the earliest known cases in mammals of what's known in evolutionary biology as Foster's, or island, rule. This rule predicts that the smaller the island, the animals that are usually the large ones will grow progressively smaller, due to a lack of resources. And the animals that are usually the smaller ones, such as rabbits, will become bigger than their diminutive peers on the mainland due to a lack of predators. Because it shared Minorca with a few bats and mice, *N. rex* had little need to expend its energy on keeping watch for predators, so could instead concentrate all its efforts on growing huge.

Microraptor Shows Its True Colors

"Strip-o-gram!"

"He's here! He's here! He's—Oh."

"You're disappointed?"

"Well I was kind of hoping for someone a little more, I don't know, *colorful*. You're sleek and sophisticated, I'll give you that, but this is a hen's night, not a fucking board meet—Oh my."

"What?"

"Your feathers just caught the light and look, I've got goosebumps . . . Why aren't you dancing!"

IN RECENT YEARS, SCIENTISTS have been developing new techniques that allow them to observe the composition of a fossilized feather down to its very molecules, which means we can finally discover the colors of the earliest birdlike creatures on Earth. In early 2012, researchers led by evolutionary biologist Ryan Carney from Brown University discovered that the feathers of the iconic birdlike dinosaur *Archaeopteryx* were structurally identical to those of modern birds. Which is pretty incredible, considering *Archaeopteryx* is 150 million years old.

The study of fossilized melanosomes—pigment granules that contain melanin, the most common light-absorbing pigment that

gives skin, feathers, hair, eyes, scales, and certain internal mem-
branes their color—is very young. Up until 2006, researchers had
been misidentifying fossilized melanosomes as bacteria due to
their similar, sausage-like shape. But then molecular paleobiologist
Jakob Vinther from Brown University identified the presence of
ancient melanosomes in the ink sac of a fossilized squid, which
opened up a whole new chapter in the study of extinct birds and
feathered dinosaurs.

In January 2012, Vinther and Carney published a paper in
Nature Communications describing the results of their examination of the molecular structure of a fossilized *Archaeopteryx*
feather. The well-preserved middle-wing feather also happened
to be the first *Archaeopteryx* specimen ever described, unearthed
in 1861 by paleontologist Hermann von Meyer near Solnhofen in
Germany. Using a method based on the one Vinther had used years
earlier, and a highly powerful type of scanning electron microscope at the Carl Zeiss Laboratory in Oberkochen, Germany, the
researchers figured out how to image individual one-micron-long
melanosomes. (There are 25.5 microns in one thousandth of an
inch.) By comparing these melanosomes to those in the feathers
of eighty-seven modern bird species, the biologists concluded that
their *Archaeopteryx* feather was likely to have been black, with a 95
percent certainty.

Because black pigmentation is packed with melanin, which is
a relatively robust polymer known to make the keratin in feathers
thicker and around 40 percent harder, the researchers suggested
that this meant *Archaeopteryx* was a well-equipped flyer. Filled
with tough, black pigment, the flight feathers were likely protected
against the motion of repetitive flight and the air particles that
would continuously whoosh past. So *Archaeopteryx* had strong,

durable feathers, but what Carney and Vinther's research couldn't answer was the question of whether it flew using powered flapping or simply gliding.

Just a few months after this paper was published, a separate research team published the results of an investigation into the color of *Microraptor*'s plumage. *Microraptor* was an exquisitely feathered, magpie-sized dinosaur with four wings and a long plume of tail feathers, living 130 million years ago in the region that is now northeastern China. The team, led by biologist Matthew Shawkey from the University of Akron in Ohio, analyzed the melanosome properties and arrangements in fossilized feathers from a previously undescribed but extremely well-preserved *Microraptor* specimen housed in the Beijing Museum of Natural History. "This type of preservation, while rare, is relatively common in fossils from this area of China," says Shawkey.

Not only did Shawkey's team find that *Microraptor* had robust, black feathers, similar to *Archaeopteryx*'s 20 million years prior, but unlike *Archaeopteryx*, these feathers were glossy like a raven's.

The way keratin, melanin, and sometimes air are layered in the microstructure of a feather determines its glossiness, or iridescence. When the researchers compared the arrangement of the melanosomes in *Microraptor*'s preserved feathers to those of more than 170 modern birds of various colors, they discovered that they were most similar to the melanosome arrangements in modern iridescent feathers. As iridescence is known to play a key role in sexual signaling and display in modern birds, Shawkey's team, who published their findings in a March 2012 issue of *Science*, suggested that the same was true for *Microraptor*. "Iridescence probably has multiple functions, but the one that is most well studied is sexual signaling," says Shawkey. "Some studies suggest that females prefer to mate with more brightly colored iridescent males, and there is considerable dimorphism (the difference in color between males and females, females being duller) in many iridescent species, suggesting sexual selection."

So *Microraptor*, draped in a glossy cloak of black, iridescent feathers that extended well beyond its tailbone, appears to have been built for sexual display, and the implications of research such as Shawkey's was not lost on Carney. "The importance of this goes beyond simple aesthetics, as the presence of iridescence in *Microraptor* provides clues as to how the dinosaur might have lived and used its plumage," he said.

What remains to be discovered is that considering *Archaeopteryx*, *Microraptor*, and a similarly small, Chinese feathered dinosaur called *Anchiornis* all had at least some dark plumage, this trait could have been present in the common ancestor of birds and their closest dinosaur relatives. "I think that's pretty reasonable," says Shawkey, "particularly given the ubiquity of melanin-based color in modern birds—literally every single clade (a group containing a species and descendants, both living and extinct) of modern birds has at least some melanin-based color."

Night Vision for Hunters

"Yeah, I mean, I get *why* we hunt at night, I do, I get it. But I can't help feeling like a bit of a serial killer, you know?"

WITH ITS SLEEK PHYSIQUE, serrated teeth, and a large, sickle-shaped claw on each hind foot, *Velociraptor* was built to kill. And new evidence suggests that this feathered carnivore would wait till nightfall before beginning the hunt.

Unlike mammals and crocodiles, all dinosaurs, birds, and some reptiles have a bony ringlike structure around the eye called a scleral ring. This helps to reinforce the structure of the eye, but can also reveal a lot about the habits of its owner, which is particularly important if they happen to be extinct. Postdoctoral researcher Lars Schmitz and vertebrate paleobiologist Ryosuke Motani from the Department of Evolution and Ecology at the University of California, Davis, figured out how to use the scleral ring to determine when a particular dinosaur was most active.

Nocturnal creatures such as the Philippine tarsier, the aye-aye, and most owls have very large eyes relative to their body size. This provides them with an increased retinal surface that can pick up as much of the very limited light available to them at night as possible. With this in mind, scientists can make the assumption that if an animal's scleral rings are thin with a wide hole in the center, it is nocturnal, as the large hole allows for a larger retina, whereas thicker scleral rings with a narrower hole in the middle would belong to an animal that is most active during the day. And those animals that tend be active during both day and night will have scleral rings somewhere in the middle. "The larger the opening, the greater the total 'amount' of light that can pass through it," says Motani. "Night-active animals need to collect more light than day-active animals so that the image formed on their retina is bright enough to stimulate the light-sensitive cells there."

Motani and Schmitz measured the size of the eye socket and the inner and outer dimensions of the scleral ring in 33 Mesozoic fossilized dinosaurs, pterosaurs, and ancestral birds from 250–65 million years ago, plus those of 164 living species to check the accuracy of the method. They developed a new computer model that takes these measurements into account, plus the evolutionary relationships of the different species, to make predictions about what stage in the day each species was likely to have been most active. The animals could be categorized as follows: diurnal (day-active), nocturnal (night-active), cathemeral (day- and night-active), and crepuscular (twilight-active). "It was known that night-active animals tended to have larger eyes than their day-active counterparts, and also that these eyes had larger pupil openings for a given eye size," says Motani. "What we did not know was if the difference between night- and day-active animal eyes was sufficiently large to allow estimation of diel (the period in a 24-hour day) activity patterns in dinosaurs."

According to the researchers, who published the results in *Science* in early 2011, measurements of the scleral rings ranged from as small as 0.4 inches in *Pterodactylus antiquus*, a small pterosaur with a 39-inch-long wingspan and a soft tissue crest on the back of its head and webbed feet, to a whopping 3.7 inches in *Saurolophus osborni*, a rare herbivorous species of duckbilled dinosaur from Canada that grew to almost 33 feet long. They reported that the latter is twice the size of the emu's scleral ring, which measures 1.4 nches, but is less than half the size of scleral rings found in giant marine reptiles called Ichthyosaurs.

They found that the majority of flying creatures in their sample, which included pterosaurs and ancestral birds such as *Archaeopteryx*, were diurnal. All herbivores, including *Diplodocus* and *Protoceratops*, were found to be cathemeral, except for the smallest analyzed herbivore, *Agilisaurus louderbacki*, an agile, beaked dinosaur that would likely dash on two legs and feed on all fours. Schmitz and Motani suggest that this trend was driven by the animals' size and diet. Herbivorous mammals exceeding a body mass of 933 pounds need about twelve hours per day to forage for food, but they must also avoid the hottest parts of the day. This means to get enough food without overheating, they often need to straddle daytime and nighttime, just like today's megaherbivores such as elephants.

But *Velociraptor* and all other terrestrial predators tested turned out to be mostly night hunters, which is the pattern seen in extant mammalian carnivores. This supports a previous study carried out in 2008 by evolutionary development biologist Martin Kundrát from Uppsala University in Sweden and Jiří Janáček, a biomathematics expert from the Institute of Physiology at the Academy of Sciences of the Czech Republic in Prague. Publishing in *Die Naturwissenschaften*, the researchers speculated that, based on the brain structure of *Conchoraptor gracilis*, this small, beaked hunter likely had excellent hearing—"an adaptation required for accurate detection of prey and/or predators under conditions of low illumination." Unfortunately, bigger carnivores such as *Tyrannosaurus rex* have not provided us with sufficiently well-preserved scleral rings, so we remain in the dark about what time of day they liked to hunt.

Horses the Size of House Cats

"What is this, a litter box? Look, I know I'm cat sized, but I'm still a horse. I have my pride. Now would you kindly move away from the cat door? I have appointments."

FIFTY MILLION YEARS AGO, horses were the size of house cats. *Sifrhippus,* the earliest known horse, first appeared in the fossil record in North America about 56 million years ago. This coincided with what's known as the Paleocene–Eocene Thermal Maximum (PETM), an extremely brief but critical time during which many of the most primitive ancestors of today's mammals appeared, including the first horses, cows, and various primates. Over the 175,000-year period of the PETM, the average global temperatures shot up by about 4–6 degrees Celsius (7–11°F), caused by a massive release of carbon dioxide into the Earth's atmosphere and oceans. About a third of all mammal species at the time shrank significantly in response to this massive climate change event—one of the most rapid warming episodes in Earth's history. *Sifrhippus* reduced its body size from just over 11 pounds in weight to no more than 8.5 pounds.

While scientists have known for a long time that animals have a tendency to be smaller in hot climates and larger in cold climates—a

133

trend known as Bergmann's rule, named after nineteenth-century German biologist Christian Bergmann, who in 1847 was one of the first people to propose it—what was unclear was whether the difference in size had to do directly with the temperature, or the availability of resources.

So a team of researchers led by Ross Secord, assistant professor in vertebrate paleontology and paleoclimatology from the University of Nebraska–Lincoln and Jonathan Bloch, associate curator of vertebrate paleontology for the Florida Museum of Natural History at the University of Florida, decided to examine the teeth of *Sifrhippus* to figure it out. "The first horse that came to North America was around the size of a small dog, like a mini schnauzer, then they immediately started to shrink to the size of a small cat. It took about 100,000 years—that's fast," says Bloch. "Various theories [exist] for why this change has happened. We've known that this interval is special, it's the first appearance of these very important mammals, so that's why I've focused on it for the past nine years. I've been trying to understand what's happening to the animals during this time."

Bloch, Secord, and colleagues had been working in the Bighorn Basin in north central Wyoming for almost ten years, examining the fossilized horse teeth from the PETM buried at the site. By analyzing the size of the teeth and the oxygen and carbon isotopes within (an isotope is a variant of a chemical element that scientists regularly use to figure out what the environment was like during a certain period of time), they teased out the progression of the ancient horse's size and the corresponding temperature of its environment. They published the results in a 2012 issue of *Science*. "What makes this really special [is] from the composition of the teeth of the mammals, we could back out the temperature that the animals lived in," says Bloch, "and were able to show how the animal changed during the time, and how the shifts in size correlated with the shift in temperature in something like a horse."

What the researchers found when they plotted the size of *Sifrhippus* through time was quite stunning—a very clear, close correlation between the temperature of the environment and the horse's sudden dip in size during the PETM, before increasing to almost 15 pounds during the following 45,000 years when the temperature returned to normal. What followed was an incredible diversification of the horse, which branched out from *Sifrhippus* into an array of species with very different histories. During the Miocene epoch, which spanned from 23 million years ago to just over 5 million years ago, the evolution of the Earth's grasslands occurred, which changed things for horses dramatically because for the first time ever, they emerged from their homes in the forest. "It's a whole different story," says Bloch. Gradually, over tens of millions of years, the tiny first horse reached the solid 1100 pounds it is today.

PART FOUR

PREY

Cliff-Diving Toad

LAUNCHING YOURSELF OFF A cliff face at the sight of a predator might look exactly like suicide, but when you're a Venezuela pebble toad this is actually the perfect getaway.

In the Guiana Highlands of South America, which run through Venezuela, Guyana, and Brazil, sheer, flat-topped pillars loom above misty cloud forests. These strange mountains, known as tepuis, are so tall and inaccessible, some reaching over half a mile above the forest floor, that they have their own unique climates and ecosystems, supporting endemic species that are found nowhere else on Earth. Multiple sinkholes 984 feet deep and 984 feet in diameter spot the surface of the tepuis, each containing their own unique species.

Venezuela pebble toads thrive on the tepuis, but it isn't easy—they can't hop or swim, and while their warty, dark grey skin camouflages them against the mountain rocks, they lack the advantage of the bright colorings that many frogs and toads use to warn predators away from eating them, whether or not they're actually poisonous. Plus at no more than 1.2 inches in length, they are also extremely small, making them the perfect snack for the tarantulas and scorpions that stalk the surface. Fortunately, these tiny bodies are the very things that keep the pebble toads alive.

When threatened by a predator, the pebble toad will roll itself into a ball and throw itself off the side of the mountain, bouncing down the rocky walls until it lands on a flat surface below. It will often tumble for many feet, but because it keeps its incredibly light body so rigid and its muscles so tense, the impact of the fall is too minor to cause it any injury. The pebble toad simply gets up and ambles away. The only time this escape strategy fails is if the pebble toad accidentally lands in a puddle that is too deep to crawl out of and it drowns.

This behavior was discovered for the first time by ecologist and director of the Coastal Plains Institute and Land Conservancy in Florida, Bruce Means, who is one of the world's foremost experts on the pebble toad. In 2009, he escorted a two-man camera crew from the BBC to the surface plateau of a tepui to film documentary footage. Means had previously observed the same behavior in the thumb-sized waterfall toads (*Oreophrynella macconnelli*) that inhabit the dense, fog-covered cloud forests that skirt the tepuis. When a predator is near, the waterfall toad will launch itself from whatever branch or leaf it is sitting on and tumble until it grabs onto something below with its oversized Mickey Mouse–esque hands and feet. Like the Venezuela pebble toad, the waterfall toad can't effectively jump, so falling is the most effective method to get far away from lurking tree snakes or spiders.

Means examined the enormous hands shared by the waterfall and pebble toads, commenting that while they're perfect for grasping onto leaves and branches during a tumble through the cloud forest, they're not so useful on the flat tepui summits. So why do the pebble toads have them at all?

The tepuis were formed over millions of years as persistent wind and rain combined with the movements of the Earth's crust to erode and elevate South America's expansive sandstone plateau. Gradually, hundreds of towering pillars were formed and the waterfall toads likely rode up with them from the cloud forests below. Over the millennia, the waterfall toads have evolved into a number of summit-dwelling pebble toad species, each suited to their own tepui's particular environment, but have retained their ancestors' most important instinct—leap or be lunch.

"I'm going to be honest, Pebble Toad, I like you for this position. But I'm a little concerned about the number of employers you've had over the past twelve months. And I can't see any position here that's lasted longer than a month. Can you explain?"

"I'm too ambitious? I'm overqualified? Hold on, let me just get my list of references for you."

"Why is your briefcase filled with dirt?"

"Okay, fine! I'm lying! I can't keep a steady job because I move around all the time. But do you have any idea how hard it is to set yourself up in a new town every time you fall down a cliff because someone wants to eat you? You see these goofy hands? You'd think I'd be able to climb back up with these, and I probably could, but it'd take me *months,* and by that stage someone else would have already moved into my house and taken my job as a movie ticket vendor because unlike me, they probably don't need to sit on ten stacked telephone directories just to see out of the booth. Do you mind if I smoke in here?"

"Mr. Toad, I'm not sure—"

"Not to mention my wife wants to know why I have so many exes posting angry comments on my Facebook wall, and my friends want to know why I never RSVP to anything anymore. And you've seen my resume. God forbid I ever try actually having a family. Leave that, they'll call you back."

"Mr. Toad, I need to take this call."

"I should probably just embrace the lifestyle, you know? Become an outlaw or something. But I couldn't steal shit because what's the point? It's not like I can take anything with me. You know my brother died last year? Fell into a puddle at the bottom of a jump. They say it was an accident, but I'm not convinced. You got any snacks?"

"Mr. Toad, I like you. I'd like to offer you this job, but—Stop! Shit. Grace! Get in here!"

"Sir? What happened to your candidate?"

"Jumped straight through the window. Damndest thing, I was about to tell him he had the job, but I couldn't offer him an office with a window."

"I'll get someone to clean up the glass."

"You're a doll."

Transformer Butterflies

"Doug, you march right back into your room and don't come out until you look disgusting. Do I *look* like I'm joking? One more 'But Mum' and you won't be going to the dance at all. I won't have you killed just because you want to impress the girls by not being disgusting."

IN APRIL 1848, HENRY Walter Bates joined fellow British naturalist, explorer, and amateur entomologist Alfred Russel Wallace in an expedition to the Amazon rainforest to solve what Bates called "the problem of the origin of the species." It was at this time that many scientists in England, including Thomas Henry Huxley, Richard Spruce, and Charles Darwin, were developing the theory of evolution by natural selection, which in its most basic form claimed that life progresses from being simple to highly complex over time.

Wallace and Bates arrived at a hut in a region of Brazil called Ega (now known as Tefe), where they split up to explore the Amazon separately. Bates worked with Amazonian butterflies for the next eleven years. Returning to London in 1859 with some 14,000 specimens, Bates, a relatively unknown scientist at the time, found himself broke. It was Darwin, who had published *On the Origin of Species* that same year, who threw him a lifeline, helping him find a job at the Royal Geological Society in 1864. In return, Bates provided Darwin with the first real evidence for natural selection, known as insect mimicry.

When Bates and Wallace were in the Amazon, they noticed that different species of butterflies were mimicking each other's wing patterns. Bates proposed that certain species of butterflies had evolved the ability to change their appearance to ward off predatory birds. Named "Batesian mimicry," this phenomenon describes the ability of a palatable species to mimic an unpalatable or noxious species.

Around the same time, German zoologist Johann Friedrich Theodor "Fritz" Müller was working with a species of long-winged brown, golden, and yellow Amazonian butterfly called the Numata longwing butterfly (*Heliconius numata*). Publishing his findings in 1878, Müller reported that the Numata longwing butterfly was able to morph into seven different wing patterns, each identical to the wing patterns of a separate group of butterflies, the toxic *Melinaea*. The difference here was that *both* species of butterflies were inedible. Müllerian mimicry reasoning poses the question: Why should prey animals employ a number of different warning signals—each of which must be learned by predators through experience—instead of everyone just using the same warning signal? If a number of prey species agree on a common warning signal, it would take predators a much shorter time to learn not to target any of them.

Exactly how butterflies are able to morph themselves into having different wing patterns took another 150 years to figure out. In 2011, scientists from France and England reported in *Nature* that they had discovered an incredible cluster of about thirty genes in a single chromosome in Numata longwing butterflies that is responsible for their mimicry. Named a "supergene," this cluster contains several genes that control the different elements of wing patterns, and the scientists found that three versions of this same chromosome coexist in the species. By changing just one gene, Numata longwing butterflies are able to look identical to another species but look completely different from each other, even though they share the same DNA.

So if these two kinds of butterflies have found success against predators in looking the same, why would they need seven different forms? Why not just use the one form of wing pattern to make things easier for predators to remember? Ecologist Mathieu Joron from France's Muséum National d'Histoire Naturelle, lead author of the *Nature* paper, suggested that each of these wing patterns has proven so successful in warning the birds and lizards away that there is not much selective pressure for the wing patterns to converge. Another possibility is that the butterflies could belong to different microhabitats, in which different patterns are more successful than others.

The team also discovered the same supergene in the peppered moth, which can be found in Europe and North America. In nineteenth-century Britain, when the industrial revolution rendered everything a sooty shade of grey, the peppered moth changed from having a light-colored wing pattern to having black wings, which allowed them to blend with their new environment.

Don't Get Angry: Vomit

EUROPEAN ROLLER
(*Coracias garrulus*)

THE SMELL OF FEAR might sound like abstract nonsense, but the phenomenon of emitting detectable odors in response to a threat spans the smallest insects to the bravest humans.

In late 2008, researchers from Stony Brook University in New York investigated the underarm secretions of twenty novice skydivers before they did their first tandem jump to see if their sweat held any clues about the human fear response. Volunteers were asked to sniff the sweat that was collected in the skydivers' clothing during the jump, plus the sweat collected while the skydivers ran on a treadmill for a similar length of time on the same day. In order to eliminate bias, the volunteers were not told what the study was about. An analysis of the volunteers' brain activity while sniffing the two types of sweat revealed that their amygdala, the brain region associated with fear memory and response, was more active when they sniffed the skydiving sweat. Publishing their findings in *PLoS ONE* the following year, the team suggested that humans have some kind of signaling system whereby emotional stress can be sensed via the chemicals that are emitted during a frightening situation.

Elsewhere in the animal kingdom, fear signals are a whole lot less subtle. There are plenty of examples in the avian world of birds that secrete certain chemicals for the specific purpose of deterring would-be predators. The northern fulmar (*Fulmarus glacialis*), a gull-like seabird from the north Atlantic and north Pacific, expels projectile stomach oils at predatory birds to mat their plumage and strip it of its waterproofing, and large, striking sea ducks called common eiders (*Somateria mollissima*) spray feces on their feet during incubation season when threatened in order to deter predators from their eggs.

But do birds ever produce a chemical response to fear that is designed to warn those of the same species of a threatening situation, rather than to deter predators? The European roller (*Coracias garrulus*) is a migratory, cavity-nesting bird whose range extends through northwest Africa, Europe, parts of the Middle East, and central Asia. Crow sized but stunningly colorful, they are adorned with iridescent kingfisher-blue plumage capped with tawny upper parts and shocks of azure along the front edge of their wings. As nestlings, they vomit pungent orange liquid on themselves when threatened.

Researchers from the Estación Experimental de Zonas Áridas in Spain decided to investigate the exact function of this vomit, to figure out if it acts simply to deter predators or to communicate a message amongst the rollers. They also wanted to discover to what degree the birds are using their sense of smell to defend themselves. After selecting a number of nests with ten-day-old nestlings inside and measuring the level of attentiveness their parents paid to them, the team painted 1 milliliter (0.2 tsp) of either roller vomit or lemon essence on the insides of the nests. By applying very similar-looking liquids, they could effectively test the birds' sense of smell.

The researchers, led by evolutionary and behavioral ecologist Deseada Parejo, reported that the parent European rollers returning to the vomit-laced nests exercised far more caution, and took much longer to settle back in. "Indeed, the supposedly defensive liquid which nestling rollers vomit when disturbed is smelled by parents so that they can adjust their behavior to avoid predation," they reported in a 2012 issue of *Royal Society Biology Letters*. So it seems that the vomit is a mechanism by which the nestlings can inform their parents of a threat that occurred while they were on a hunting trip. A further advantage of the vomit could be that it makes the nestlings undesirable food for predators, which in turn increases the parents' chance of survival.

Don't think I can't see what's really going on here, European roller nestlings. Sure, it *looks* like a clever survival mechanism, but as if you're not just trying to cover yourselves for all the ridiculous parties you have in your nest while your parents are out finding food. *For you,* nestlings. Wait, you're not? Why wouldn't you?

Think about it: One night you'll all be like, "Quick, Steve: are your parents gone yet? Get the hell over here, we're playing strip poker!"

And Steve will be like, "Wow I didn't know anyone *actually* plays strip poker. Definitely not interested in that, Multiple Joeys from *Friends*."

ZING, nestlings!

So you'll have to wait till your parents go out *again* to try to throw your amazingly cool party, and this time you'll actually follow the number one rule when it comes to throwing amazingly cool parties according to every teen movie ever—you need to supply the alcohol. And then all you'll need to do when your parents call and say they're on their way home is tell everyone that you're running out of alcohol so they'd better drink whatever they can get their hands on real quick. And then, nestlings, just sit back and wait for the vomits to arrive.

This will buy you some valuable time, because your parents will have to wait it out at some bar because of the "predators," so you can keep trying to hit on Steve's little sister and all her friends. Although they have all just vomited on themselves, nestlings, so it depends on how desp—Oh. Almost forgot who I was talking to for a second.

Poison-Blood–Spitting Eyes

TEXAS HORNED LIZARD
(Phrynosoma cornutum)

"All right, so I don't care if you're handsome or smart or even nice at this point. But let's just get a few things straight. If we *do* end up in a relationship, there will be no surprise parties, no unannounced tickle fights—or announced ones for that matter—and when I have the hiccups, for god's sake don't try any 'fright' tactics. Unless you think a girl shooting blood out of her eyes is a turn-on, in which case we might have something (but we won't, because I'm not interested in creeps). If you think all of that sounds reasonable, let's do coffee. Oh, and must hate dogs. x"

"Hi Texas Horned Lizard, you look cute in your profile pic, where is that, Kansas? Anyway, I don't want to sound presumptuous, but I think we could get along pretty great. I do gross things with my ribs when I'm scared and I'm embarrassed about it too, so let's just drink tea and watch *Seinfeld* and play board games. The least scary date in the world. And if the neighbor's dog suddenly barks, or the wind slams a door shut, or my idiot housemate turns a blender on in the kitchen without warning, my ribs will explode and you'll shoot blood out of your eyes, and we'll laugh about it and then have more tea. That doesn't sound too bad, right? Spanish Ribbed Newt. xo"

WITH A BLUNT FACE framed by a halo of horns and a flattened, tanklike body, the Texas horned lizard (*Phrynosoma cornutum*) looks like a tiny dragon. With the biggest males growing to almost 4 inches in length, it is the largest of the fourteen species of horned lizard spread across the western United States and Mexico, and is one of three horned lizard species that can shoot jets of poison blood from its eye sockets when threatened.

Known as "autohemorrhaging" or "reflex bleeding," this behavior is exceptionally rare in vertebrates. The only other known species to do it are *Tropidophis*, a dwarf boa that squirts blood from its mouth, nostrils, and eyes, and *Natrix natrix*, a grass snake that secretes blood from its mouth and nose to convincingly play dead when faced with a predator.

The Texas horned lizard autohemorrhages to both confuse and ward off predators such as coyotes, hawks, and domestic dogs. It obtains its poison from a diet of insects, specifically harvester ants (*Pogonomyrmex*), which carry one of the most toxic natural venoms known in the world. This means the lizard has had to evolve a complex method of capturing and swallowing these ants so they don't harm its mouth, pharynx, or stomach with their venom.

In 2008, Wade C. Sherbrooke, director of the Southwestern Research Station at the American Museum of Natural History in New York and Kurt Schwenk, professor of ecology and evolutionary biology at the University of Connecticut, published the results of an examination of some road-killed Texas horned lizards in the *Journal of Experimental Zoology*. The pair opened the lizards' stomachs to find that they were packed with dozens of poisonous *Pogonomyrmex* ants. Sherbrooke and Schwenk discovered that mucus-secreting papillae, which are the little fleshy projections that line the back end of the horned lizard's tongue and the pharynx, are the key to their survival against the venomous ants. The papillae squeeze and bind the ants in mucus strands as they are swallowed—and never chewed—and once they reach the esophagus, the ants are met with specialized mucus-secreting skin folds that ensure they are incapacitated all the way down to the stomach.

In mid-2010, Sherbrooke revisited his Texas horned lizard research with biologist William Cooper of Indiana University-Purdue University to test if a hypothesis known as "escape theory" applies to a species so good at camouflaging itself. Escape theory predicts that once an animal has detected a predator nearby, it will not flee immediately, but wait and monitor the predator's approach, weighing up the risk of getting caught versus the cost of fleeing from its current location where food foraging and mating opportunities may exist. If an animal does decide to flee, its level of fitness will determine the initial distance left between it and its predator—a space known as "flight initiation distance." The fitter the prey, the shorter the distance left between it and the predator before the prey takes off. What the researchers found when observing the Texas horned lizard was that the individuals who were alone when spotted by a predator had an average flight initiation distance almost twice as long as those who were in the company of other lizards and interacting socially with them. They were reluctant to flee so quickly when potential mates were present, and are thus living proof of escape theory.

"Hi Spanish Ribbed Newt, how's this Thursday sound? I'll bring Scrabble. x"

Will Rib You to Death

IN 1879, GERMAN ZOOLOGIST and comparative anatomist Franz von Leydig noticed some very odd behavior in a rather unassuming species of newt. When provoked, the Spanish ribbed newt's ribs will burst out of its skin to produce twin rows of poison-tipped spears, perfect for fending off anything that was considering taking a bite out of it. But it would take 130 years before scientists had the technology to explain just how an animal can wield its own skeleton as a weapon.

Also known as the Iberian ribbed newt, the water-loving Spanish ribbed newt grows to 12 inches long and is endemic to Morocco and the central and Iberian Peninsula, which runs through Spain, Portugal, and Andorra. It has a flat head and a slender tail measuring half the length of its body and a row of rust-colored tubercules, or warts, that run down each side where the ribs protrude.

In a 2009 paper published by the *Journal of Zoology*, zoologist Egon Heiss of the University of Vienna in Austria and colleagues reported what they saw using a combination of photographic and X-ray imaging and computed tomography (CT) scans. They discovered that when agitated, this newt is able to swing its long ribs forward by up to 65 degrees while keeping the rest of its body still. This causes its ribs to end up at a perpendicular (90 degree) angle to the spine, piercing through the skin on the side of its torso. The Spanish ribbed newt manages this grisly party trick because of its peculiar anatomy. Each of its hollow, spear-shaped ribs is attached to its corresponding vertebra by a flexible two-headed joint that allows it to be swung forward independently of the rest of the body.

Being mostly small and soft, amphibians have had to evolve many different kinds of defense mechanisms in order to survive, and one of the most common of these is secreting venom through the pores on their skin. The Spanish ribbed newt combines its defense mechanisms by secreting a noxious, milky substance onto its skin when threatened, which coats the exposed rib points to inflict a series of painful, stinging jabs. What particularly surprised Heiss was that the species appears to be immune to the pain of repeatedly piercing its bones through its skin, observing that "the skin in the penetration areas lacks permanent pores through which the ribs could be projected."

A powerful immune system seems to protect the newt's wounds from becoming infected while its skin works at regenerating itself through a process called cell dedifferentiation. Cell differentiation sees a stem cell develop into a more specialized type of cell, such as a bone or blood cell, whereas dedifferentiation means a specialized cell will revert to its primitive form, often for the purpose of regeneration. In the newt's case, the cells around the puncture wounds dedifferentiate, multiplying rapidly and differentiating again to create new skin cells. This process also applies to limbs and other organs, which newts are known to be able to regenerate multiple times over.

What a couple of dinner guests Texas Horned Lizard and Spanish Ribbed Newt would make.

Mr. and Mrs. Bullfrog will be in their kitchen before they arrive and Mrs. Bullfrog will be like, "I don't know why you invited them, I only just had the carpet steam-cleaned after the last time . . ."

"They reimbursed you for it though."

"That's not the point. It's a hassle, and I bet there are still blood molecules in the fibers."

"Blood molecules. Jesus."

The pair will arrive, looking typically nervous, and they'll all sit down in the living room with a bottle of wine while Spanish Ribbed Newt silently measures the distance between himself and every object in the room that could fall on him. Or that he could fall into. And he'll decide to crouch in the corner on the floor because that will give him the biggest head start should the couch or the grandfather clock decide to charge at him or something. Texas Horned Lizard will look embarrassed about it, but she'll be the one carrying industrial-strength carpet cleaner in her handbag.

She'll tell the Bullfrogs about her promotion at work and Mr. Bullfrog will be all, "This calls for champagne!" and Texas Horned Lizard and Spanish Ribbed Newt will simultaneously say *"No champagne"* exactly like how two people say it in a sitcom when they're hiding a hilarious secret.

"Since when?"

"We were at a restaurant last week and someone unexpectedly popped a champagne cork behind us and we practically shat ourselves.

I got blood all over the tablecloth and Spanish Ribbed Newt put a waiter in the hospital. It was very embarrassing."

"He was standing too close and got a rib in his thigh," Spanish Ribbed Newt will mutter to the carpet.

Mrs. Bullfrog will show everyone into the dining room. "Spanish Ribbed Newt, you're over there next to Mr. Bullfrog, and Texas Horned Lizard, you're on this side with me." Dinner will begin pretty smoothly, except for one minor hiccup when Mrs. Bullfrog will startle everyone by accidentally dropping her knife on her plate with a loud *clang*, and Texas Horned Lizard will nervously joke about her carpet cleaner.

But Spanish Ribbed Newt will be looking down at his exposed ribs under the tablecloth with a silent and intense expression of horror. "Shit. Oh shit. Oh shit. Ohhh shit. Erm, Mr Bullfrog . . ." But then he'll think better of it, put his skeleton back in, and pour himself another glass of wine.

"So I was like, 'Hey, Johnson in accounts, Alex Perry called, he wants his botox back—' Ughhh."

"What, honey?"

"I suddenly feel *terrible*. Oh god . . ."

Spanish Ribbed Newt will quickly drag Texas Horned Lizard to the door, all like, "Keep moving, I'll explain on the way!" while Mr. Bullfog's moans get louder and more gurgly. Then he'll remove his waistcoat. "Hey, what are these hole—"

Thud.

Playing Dead Pros

VIRGINIA OPOSSUM
(Didelphis virginiana)

THE SWEET LITTLE VIRGINIA opossum not only has a well-stocked bag of tricks to get itself out of a sticky situation, it's also forcing venomous snakes to up their game.

The opossum is one of the most primitive living ancestors of marsupials and has remained morphologically unchanged for the past 60 million years, despite dramatic habitat changes. The only marsupial in North America, it made its way from South America during what scientists consider to be one of the most significant geologic events in the last 60 million years. A volcanic strip of land known as the Isthmus of Panama rose up out of the ocean as two of the Earth's plates slowly collided 15 million years ago, and gradually the Central American Seaway that separated North and South America was filled in completely 3 million years ago. Not only did this rearrangement of the Earth's terrestrial regions have a significant impact on its climate and environment, it also profoundly changed the biodiversity of the Americas.

Known as the Great American Interchange, this period saw the ancestors of South American animals such as the armadillo, sloth, porcupine, anteater, and opossum migrate to North America, and the ancestors of bears, cats, pigs, dogs, and horses journey in the opposite direction. Much later, the Virginia opossum, which was native to the eastern United States, was introduced to the West during the Great Depression in the early twentieth century as a source of food.

Looking just like a sneakier version of Mickey Mouse, the Virginia opossum has a long snout that tapers to a pastel pink nose, dark, beady eyes framed by a snow-white face, and black, rounded ears. They share their habitat with the huge population of cats and dogs in the United States, so can only survive with the help of the many defenses that render them undesirable to predators. When threatened, they will stand their ground, open their mouths wide, and expose an array of pointy teeth. If this gaping leer doesn't ward off the predator and the opossum can't escape the situation by fleeing, it will suddenly, and very convincingly, play dead.

Named after the Greek word for "putting to death," *thanatosis* describes the process of an animal, insect, bird, or reptile going into a comatose state in the face of danger, which can often work in its favor, because limp, immobile prey is nowhere near as fun to play with as struggling, terrified prey. The Virginia opossum will fall to its side with its body flexed, mouth agape, and heart rate, respiratory rate, and body temperature rapidly decreasing. And to make things just a little bit more authentic, the *thanatosis* is accompanied by excessive drooling, urination, and the excretion of droppings and greenish, foul-smelling anal fluid. Sometimes the males will even have an erection. Chances are that the predator will assume the opossum is extremely sick or dead, and its instincts will tell it to keep away for the sake of its own health.

There have even been suggestions that the Virginia opossum somehow remains conscious during *thanatosis*. "Several authors have raised the question of consciousness during paralysis in animals. Our opossums appeared aware of their assailant during paralysis," Geir Wing Gabrielsen, a senior research scientist in zoo physiology from the Institute of Medical Biology University of Tromsø in Norway wrote in his 1985 paper published by *Acta*

Physiologica Scandinavica. "We observed a delay in recovery as long as the dog was present or the opossum was touched by man. During paralysis in ducks, the birds similarly appeared alert and aware of escape opportunities. They also seemed to distinguish between approaches by foxes and humans."

More recently, scientists have investigated another of the Virginia opossum's talents—its invulnerability to snake venom. The Virginia opossum is known to eat rattlesnakes, copperhead pit viper snakes, and some species of tropical pit vipers called lanceheads. These snakes all wield a powerful type of venom made up of dozens of toxic compounds that can cause massive internal hemorrhaging. Publishing in *PLoS ONE* in 2011, researchers from the American Museum of Natural History in New York suggested that the opossum's resistance to viper venom is driving the substance's rapid evolution. They discovered this by sequencing several opossum genes, including one that had been discovered in a previous study to code for a vital blood-clotting protein called the von Willebrand factor (vWF), which many snake-venom toxins target. Once they started to analyze the data, the researchers found that vWF was an outlier, evolving far more quickly than predicted, forcing the viper venom toxins to keep up by evolving just as quickly.

"Most herpetologists interpret this as evidence that venom in snakes evolves because of interactions with their prey, but if that were true, you would see equally rapid evolution in toxin-targeted molecules of prey species, which has not yet been seen," said one of the researchers, Robert Voss, curator in the Department of Mammalogy at the American Museum of Natural History. "What we've found is that a venom-targeted protein is evolving rapidly in mammals that eat snakes. So it looks like the snake venom is evolving according to its dual roles—feeding and defense—and the snake-eating Virginia opossum is the force driving it."

Well now, there's a genius way of getting out of any situation ever, huh, Virginia Opossum? I bet you're one of those guys who take a million sick days off work just because you can, while the rest of us have to sweat over our overly elaborate lies because we're cursed with terrific immune systems.

But this kind of attitude can backfire on you, Virginia Opossum. Seriously. You'll arrive at the office after another one of your "sick days" and realize you missed cake from Badger's birthday, and everyone will be like, "Oh man, you missed some really good cake yesterday." And then one of the interns will pipe up and say that actually, this is kind of embarrassing, but it's her birthday today, and everyone will be like, "More cake!" And you'll be 'Oh my god, cake!' at the same time, but then one of your coworkers—the me-equivalent who knows you're full of shit—will be all, "Do you really think it's a good idea to have cake so soon after you fainted and shat all over the carpet? Something is clearly not right with your bowels, Virginia Opossum, and cake is certainly not going to help."

So then it will be cake time and everyone will have to stop what they're doing and stand around the cake table, *so awkwardly*, Virginia Opossum, making small talk about how good the cake is for however long it takes before someone—most likely the me-equivalent—decides to sit back down because their work isn't going to do itself. And imagine how much more awkward that situation would be for you, Virginia Opossum, because you won't even have a piece of cake to stare down into and compare its deliciousness level to that of last week's or yesterday's cake.

But I guess of course you can always get out of the situation in the same way you get out of every situation and lapse into a pungent coma, but just know that the me-equivalent will be licking the ends of all your pens and farting on your keyboard before you're even halfway home.

Underwater Mousedeer

"Seriously, Chevrotain, get out of the water. There's no one here."

"No, no, I'm fine where I am. It's cool. We can play like this. Someone roll for me."

"You landed on Pall Mall. Do you want it?"

"Want *what*?"

"PALL MALL."

"Pall *what*? Oh, right. No, I'll leave it."

"WHAT?'"

"NO THANKS, I'LL LEAVE IT."

"CAN'T HEAR Y—"

"I DON'T. WANT. IT."

"I'm having the worst time."

"WHAT?"

ALSO KNOWN AS A mousedeer, the chevrotain is a nimble, cat-sized mammal with a round, stocky body perched on delicate legs and hooves. It couldn't look less suited to a life underwater, but its peculiar habit of submerging itself when threatened mirrors the evolutionary transition from terrestrial mammals to primitive whales.

Around 50 million years ago, the chevrotains split from the rest of the ruminants, which are a large group of herbivores including giraffes, cattle, antelopes, and goats that regurgitate their semi-digested food and chew it as cud. They evolved differently—most ruminants have four-chambered stomachs whereas chevrotains have three-chambered stomachs—and separated into their own family called Tragulidae. There are now ten species of chevrotain in the world, found in Africa and Asia, and the water chevrotain (*Hyemoschus aquaticus*), also known as the fanged deer, is the largest and most primitive.

Until recently, it was assumed that chevrotains, like the deer they look so much like, were unequivocally land mammals, but a couple of chance sightings changed everything. In 2008, a group of researchers led by ecologist Erik Meijaard from the Nature Conservancy in Indonesia carried out a biodiversity survey in the Central Kalimantan Province of Borneo. They passed a greater Malay chevrotain (*Tragulus napu*) swimming in one of the forest streams. When it spotted the researchers, the startled chevrotain dove underwater and stayed submerged for an entire hour, briefly coming up for oxygen five or six times. Even more remarkable than its ability to stay underwater for multiple five-minute stretches, the particular chevrotain was able to do it while pregnant. The researchers confirmed what the Borneo locals had been saying for years—that the strange little chevrotains tend to head straight for the nearest creek or river to escape their dogs.

That same year, Meijaard and colleagues investigated a single chevrotain in Sri Lanka that submerged itself in a pond to escape a brown mongoose, describing its swimming behavior in *Mammalian Biology*:

> The mongoose did not enter the water but at times approached within two metres (*6.5 feet*) of the mousedeer, which responded by flaring its throat and showing the white on its throat. The

mountain mousedeer (or chevrotain) swam with only the upper half of its head out of the water and was completely submerged at times.

After fifteen minutes, the chevrotain emerged, only to be chased straight back in by the tenacious mongoose. "Investigation revealed that, similar to the Bornean specimen, this was also a pregnant female," the team revealed.

The researchers also pointed out that while the chevrotains are not closely related to modern whales, their submerging behavior offers an analogue to another water-friendly hoofed mammal that lived millions of years ago.

Since Darwin speculated more than 150 years ago in *On the Origin of Species*, scientists have accepted that modern whales are the ancestors of terrestrial mammals, and over the past fifteen years, a number of intermediate fossils have been discovered that document this evolutionary journey from land to sea. One of the most significant of these discoveries occurred in 2007, when a team led by Hans Thewissen, a professor of anatomy from the Northeastern Ohio Universities Colleges of Medicine and Pharmacy, unearthed the 48-million-year-old bones of a genus of ancient, water-loving deerlike mammals called *Indohyus*. According to Thewissen, the fact that the chevrotain family Tragulidae had originally belonged to an ancient family of ruminants called Ruminantia indicated that aquatic escape is a behavior with very deep roots in hoofed land mammals.

A Poisonous Pelt

AFRICAN CRESTED RAT
(Lophiomys imhausi)

THE AFRICAN CRESTED RAT might look exactly like a kind of cuddly porcupine, but thanks to a neat little trick it's learned, it's a whole lot more dangerous.

No actual relation to rats, the African crested, or "maned," rat can grow up to 21 inches from head to tail, and gives birth to fully furred young. Found in East African countries such as Ethiopia, Somalia, Kenya, and Tanzania, the crested rat is named after its distinctive coat of long, dense fur, silver and black tipped in color with a thick grey and white undercoat. Its fur features a long crest of coarse, black-and-white banded hairs running along its back from its nape to the base of its tail, and on either side of the crest are strips of shorter, chestnut-colored hairs that cover an area of glandular skin. When aggravated, the African crested rat will pull its head into its shoulders and use special muscles to part this peculiar area of fur and expose the skin beneath, pointing it toward a predator as if to say, "bite me." This behavior is so unlike that of any other prey animal, who would either flee or try to at least protect its vulnerable flesh from a predator, that scientists have struggled to explain it since the species' discovery in 1867.

Some scientists thought that the ability to draw attention to its striking black-and-white mane was a form of mimicry, the crested rat making itself appear like a porcupine or a zorilla—skunk-like polecats that emit foul-smelling secretions to make themselves seem less appetizing to predators. The crested rat's apparent impersonation of the polecat was said to be a form of Batesian mimicry, a technique that describes a defenseless, naturally sluggish animal copying the defense mechanism of another animal in the face of danger. But then reports of dogs biting crested rats and then rapidly dying of heart failure began to surface, and it was clear that something else was in play.

In mid-2011, scientists from the University of Oxford published a paper in *Proceedings of the Royal Society* announcing that they had finally solved the puzzle of the African crested rat. They discovered that the species takes advantage of the highly toxic poison arrow tree (*Acokanthera schimperi*) by chewing on its bark and roots and smearing the toxins along its mane. African hunters use this toxin, called ouabain, to produce poison-tipped arrows that can bring down something as powerful as an elephant. According to the researchers, this particular defense technique is unique among the 4000 known species of placental mammals. A similar example of this behavior exists in the hedgehog, which chews on the poison glands of toads and slathers the venom on its spines. But the worst this can do is make a prick from its spines slightly more painful, and unlike the African crested rat's poisonous fur, has never resulted in a recorded death.

A chemical analysis of the crested rat's hairs revealed that they are loaded with ouabain, which works by inhibiting the pump that controls the balance of sodium and potassium ions in the body's cells. This causes the cells to be flooded with sodium and calcium ions, and even small doses of ouabain can lead to muscle contractions. Higher doses can lead to deadly respiratory or cardiac arrest. The researchers tested the reaction of the flank hairs when brought into contact with liquid, in this case red ink, under a microscope. They discovered that each shaft is covered in tiny holes that eagerly soaked up the ink, while the fine fibers loaded inside each shaft effectively hold the substance in place. Thanks to its specialized flank hairs, the African crested rat is a poison-soaking and storing machine. What remains a mystery is how it prevents itself from being poisoned as it chews the bark of the poison arrow tree, when a tiny amount can bring a hippo or an elephant to its knees.

"Look, I get it, African Crested Rat, but I just don't think it's going to work."

"Can I show you my sketches?"

"Okay, show me your sketches."

"So here's African Crested Rat Man fighting a house cat in his underground lair."

"What's that?"

"That's African Crested Rat Man's utility belt."

"What's in it?"

"Nothing."

"Pardon?"

"There's nothing in it. That's the point. We don't have to *do* anything, we just have to stand there and show the predators our poison fur and that's our superpower."

"And you can also chew poison bark and not die."

"We'd rather not reveal the source of our powers, thanks very much."

"Okay, look, I'm going to be straight with you, African Crested Rat. I just don't think a superhero whose superpower is to *stand there and expose himself* is going to take off. Now get the hell out of my office."

What Big Eyes You Have!

GIANT AND COLOSSAL SQUID
(*Architeuthis and Mesonychoteuthis*)

"Hello?"

"Hey, it's me."

"Oh hey, Giant Squid. What do you want? I'm trying to get dressed for work over here."

"I know, I'm watching you."

"Argh, would you quit it with that stuff? You guys should have to apply for a license to see so far away. You're all a bunch of creeps."

"That's a really ugly tie."

WHILE THE DIMINUTIVE PHILIPPINE tarsier has the largest eyes relative to body size of all the mammals on Earth, the giant and colossal squid have the largest eyes of the whole animal kingdom. What scientists couldn't figure out until recently was why.

With bodies that grow up to 33 feet long from head to tentacle tip, the giant and colossal squid don't have a wealth of predators to keep watch for. Plus they share the pelagic depths—or "open sea" near neither the ocean floor nor the shore—with many animals who get by perfectly well with eyes that are a mere fraction of the size. While scientists could not figure out why these two types of squid would need eyes 10–16 inches in diameter, which is nearly three times the diameter of any other animal's eye, they knew this enormous size would have to serve a very specific function.

In 2007, the largest intact squid ever dredged up from the ocean depths was netted in the Ross Sea, a deep bay just off Antarctica. The 26-foot-long, 1091-pound adult colossal squid (*Mesonychoteuthis hamiltoni*) had stunning 11-inch-wide eyes, and it was these that a team of scientists, led by biologist Sönke Johnsen from Duke University in the United States, investigated in order to discover the secret of these mighty sea creatures and their slightly smaller cousin, the giant squid (*Architeuthis*). "Compared to the next largest eyes, they're three times wider and have twenty-seven times the volume," says Johnsen. "Like elephant trunks and the stars on star-nosed moles, you just can't help wondering what they're good for and why they look the way they do."

The team used a mathematical model to figure out the value of basketball-sized eyes in terms of vision. "Most of the research was really an extended and complex mathematical argument. And I do mean argument, since we disagreed on many points at first," says Johnsen. "A wonderful thing about studying vision in the ocean though is that the system is complex enough to give you interesting results, but simple enough that you can model it accurately." What they discovered was that the enormous output of energy to grow and maintain the eyes significantly outweighed the general vision benefits. So assuming that giant and colossal squid do what everyone else in the ocean does at depths of 984–3281 meters below the surface, their eyes would be a waste, an evolutionary blunder. But what sets these squid apart from other creatures in the ocean, and what renders these eyes an evolutionary success, is that colossal and giant squid are a favorite meal of the 49-foot-long sperm whale, judging from several stomach content analyses.

When sperm whales dive up to 1640 feet below the surface, emitting sonar to locate the whereabouts of huge squid, they set off a wave of bioluminescence from smaller gelatinous animals such as plankton wherever they go. While the giant and colossal squid's eyes don't give them significantly better eyesight, they do allow these animals to take in much more light than animals with smaller eyes. This enables them to detect the subtle differences in contrast within the dim environment of the deep sea, such as that caused by a sudden path of light emitted by smaller creatures fluorescing when disturbed by something bigger. Johnsen explains:

> The interaction of light with matter (for example a retina) is not continuous, but instead comes in discrete chunks we call photons. These arrive randomly over time, so you need a lot of them to get a sample accurate enough to see small differences in brightness between a target and the background. So having a huge eye (in particular a giant pupil) lets in more light so more photons arrive over a shorter period of time and give you a better image.

The ability to sense contrast in ocean light is not particularly useful to smaller sea creatures, who have to worry more about predators in their immediate area, but to be able to detect the presence of a giant object lurking more than 300 feet away is a matter of life and death for a giant or colossal squid. "The most likely explanation for the unusually large eyes in giant and colossal squid is the unique ability to detect large predators that trigger plankton bioluminescence as they move through the water," the researchers reported in a 2012 issue of *Current Biology*. "A long detection range implies that a huge water volume around the squid can be monitored for predators."

But being able to detect sperm whales up to 395 feet away doesn't mean that the giant and colossal squid can easily slip away undetected. The sperm whale's sonar, which the squid are incapable of hearing, will have already given away the squid's location, leading Johnsen's team to suggest that the squid's large, powerful bodies are built for hauling them and their giant eyes away from a looming threat. So the main advantage of their huge eyes is not to spot the sperm whales before the sperm whales spot them, it's to give them enough time to prepare an effective escape. "What a big eye gives you is the ability to see very low contrast objects in dim light. Where it really matters is when you are trying to see a very large object from far away underwater in dim light. Very few animals need to do this," says Johnsen. He adds:

> Whales would be the obvious choice, but they mostly use sonar and vision is relatively unimportant. So you're left with animals that are preyed upon by large toothed whales. Most of these are too small to benefit from seeing the whale, but squid are big enough to take advantage of early detection, since they actually have a chance to jump out of the way.

According to Johnsen, the only other known evolution of huge eyes is in the ichthyosaurs—a group of large sea creatures not unlike swordfish that lived around 230–100 million years ago, from the mid-Triassic to mid-Cretaceous period. These are the only animals known to have eyes comparable to the giant and colossal squids' in terms of size, which suggests that they were used to detect the presence of giant apex predators called pliosaurs. Just like the giant and colossal squids' eyes, the ichthyosaur's massive peepers would have given it the head start it needed.

Wolverine Frog

HAIRY FROG OF CAMEROON
(*Trichobatrachus robustus*)

"She left me."

"Texas Horned Lizard? For whom?"

"A fucking frog. He's got bone claws . . . I just can't believe it's over."

"Wow, she's really got a thing for species that weaponize their own skeletons, huh?"

A CREATURE THAT FLICKS claws made from its own bones through its fingers as a defense mechanism? Sure, Marvel revealed that Wolverine's six retractable claws were made from his own bones in 1993, but the hairy frog of Cameroon has been using its own bones as weapons for way longer than that.

The hairy frog of Cameroon belongs to the Arthroleptidae family of "screecher frogs" from sub-Saharan Africa, so-called because of the distinctive high-pitched call that runs through all seventy species in this group. The hairy frog is a dark-colored, almost black species with blush-pink and white colorings on its underside. At 4 inches long from snout to toe, it is among the larger of the Arthroleptidae frogs, and was named because of the odd, hair-thin skin fibers that form a thick, shaggy fur across the thighs and flanks of the males during the breeding season. Because these fibers are highly vascularized, which means they're packed with blood vessels to aid the supply of blood and oxygen, scientists have suspected that the male's hirsute coat increases respiration while it sits submerged in a stream for long periods of time on clutches of eggs laid by its mate.

While the males' hairy legs might be the most obvious physical feature of the hairy frog of Cameroon, their bone-claws are certainly the strangest. Observations have been made about claw-wielding frogs since the 1930s, the most famous of which was made by British naturalist, zookeeper, and author Gerard Durrell, who in his 1954 book *The Bafut Beagles* describes in painstaking detail the process of catching one of these nimble amphibians. And the even bigger challenge? Holding on to it.

> He was not going to give up his liberty without a fight, and he uttered a loud screaming gurk, and kicked out frantically with his free hind leg, scraping his toes across the back of my hand. As he did so, I felt as though it had been scratched with several needles, and on the skin of the back of my hand appeared several deep grooves which turned red with the welling blood. I was so astonished at this unexpected attack from a creature which I had thought to be completely harmless, that I must have relaxed my hold slightly. The frog gave an extra hard kick and a wriggle, his moist leg slid through my fingers, there was a plop as he hit the water and the ripples danced. My Hairy Frog had escaped.

The hairy frog of Cameroon shares the bone-claw trait with another species from Cameroon called *Scotobleps gabonicus,* and eleven species in the closely related *Astylosternus,* or "night frogs," genus. But despite the fact that several species of frogs wield claws, for years scientists could not explain the anatomical mechanism that causes it, because very few observations had been made using live specimens. This was until evolutionary biologist David

Blackburn from the University of Kansas Biodiversity Institute traveled to Cameroon in 2006. "I was working in Cameroon on dissertation research when I also had the experience of collecting these frogs and having them rake their claws against my skin. It's definitely enough to give you a bloody scratch and certainly can cause you to drop the frog, especially if you're not expecting it!" Blackburn says of his first encounter with the frogs.

When he returned to Harvard's Museum of Comparative Zoology, where he was based at the time, Blackburn discovered that the very claws that made him bleed in Cameroon were protruding cleanly through the toe flesh of the museum's preserved hairy frog specimens. "When discussing this with my friend and colleague [and Harvard paleontologist] Farish Jenkins, it struck us as strange that no one had ever investigated how it was that these toe bones could come to protrude through the skin," he says.

It took almost a year before Blackburn had access to enough live specimens to rule out the possibility that the hairy frog's toe claws are formed by bones that grow so long over an extended period of time that they eventually poke through the tips of the skin. Rather, he says, it seems to occur suddenly to cause a traumatic wound to the toe. "We thought it noteworthy that most vertebrates do a perfectly good job of keeping their skeletons on the inside of their bodies, and yet these frogs seemed to have evolved some mechanism for getting the last bone in their toe to pop through the skin," he says, adding that if you take a moment to look down at your own fingertips or toes and imagine somehow pushing your bones right through them on command, you can understand how strange and difficult to explain this situation was.

What he discovered is that the hairy frog of Cameroon has a small piece of bone beyond the end of the toe bones in its hind feet.

There is a soft tissue connection made of collagen that connects this little piece of bone to the end of the toe bone. It appears that when these frogs flex a particular muscle in their toe, the toe bone breaks free of this little piece of bone and pierces through the bottom of the toe. "These frogs have evolved a suite of very unusual anatomical structures at the ends of their toes. Imagine having another bit of bone beyond the last bone in your finger or toe . . . a very unusual situation!" he says, having published his findings in a 2009 issue of *Biology Letters.*

What remains to be discovered is whether or not the bone-claws of the hairy frog are retractable. Do the frogs get one shot at pushing their bones through their skin in an emergency, or can they somehow fit them back inside the tips of their toes while their skin grows back over the top? And does puncturing their own flesh like this hurt? "We need to do some basic experiments with living animals to figure this out," says Blackburn.

Bomb-Dropping Worm

SWIMA WORM
(*Swima bombiviridis*)

"I'd like to check in please. Flying to New York."

"Sure thing, sir, I just need your passpor—Wait, is this some kind of joke? Are those things *real*?"

"Look, I am *begging* you, this is the seventeenth airline I've tried, and every time I come to catch my flight I leave these things at home, but they grow back so fast, I can't control it. I just want to see my niece get christened, that's all I want to do."

"Security!"

"Okay, okay, don't bother. Look, I'm throwing myself out. But these tickets had better be refund—Okay, okay, I'm going!"

WITH JUST 9 PERCENT of the ocean's species discovered so far, we have no idea how weird things really get down there. But every new species gives us a hint that life on the land is nowhere near as bizarre.

In 2009, a handful of new deep-sea worm species was discovered off the west coast of the United States thanks to a remotely operated submersible vehicle that was patrolling the ocean between 1 and 2.3 miles below the surface. The research team behind the discovery, led by marine biologist Karen Osborn from the Scripps Institution of Oceanography at the University of California in San Diego, identified seven previously unknown species, including a swima, or bomb-dropping, worm called *Swima bombiviridis*, which sports eight "bomblike" appendages attached to the segments behind its head. "We found a whole new group of fairly large, extraordinary animals that we never knew anything about before," says Osborn. "These are not rare animals. Often when we see them they number in the hundreds. What's unique is that their habitat is really hard to sample."

Transparent, eyeless swima worms range in size from 0.7 to 3.7 inches, and their gelatinous bodies are transparent except for a bright orange gut area and the light green bombs. When agitated or threatened, the bombs—or pinhead-sized sacs filled with bioluminescent liquid—are released, and burst into a bright green light that glows for several seconds as they float away. One or two bombs are released at a time and are automatically replaced by the swima worm's body. According to Osborn, who published a description of the worms in *Science* two years following the discovery, the bombs are likely to be a defense mechanism rather than a courting device as they are used by both juvenile and adult worms alike. Because light is so limited in the deep sea where they live, the glowing bombs could function as a predator distraction while the worm escapes into the darkness.

Judging by the position of the bombs and the fact that they are so easily detachable, the researchers think they may have evolved from gills, as their ancestors' gills are positioned in exactly the same place. "The gills can fall off very easily so there's a similarity of being detachable, but for some reason the gills have transformed to become these glowing little detachable spheres," says coauthor and curator of Scripps Benthic Invertebrate Collection Greg Rouse.

The swima worms are not only well equipped for distracting predators, they're also very skilled swimmers. They're flanked by fans of long bristles that form swimming paddles that allow them to move both forwards and backwards, and the large surface area of the fans is perfect for propelling them through the water at a fast pace.

In late 2010, Osborn described the swima worms' slower, less weaponized relative called the squidworm (*Teuthidodrilus samae*). This blue and yellow creature looks like a combination of a swima worm and a squid, with ten slender tentacles protruding from its head. Two of the tentacles are yellow and curled loosely like a corkscrew, which Osborn suggests are used for feeding. The remaining eight blue tentacles are likely used for breathing, and could also help the squidworm feel its way around in the dark. Like the swima worm, the squidworm's body is also lined with an array of bristles, but it tends to swim at a more leisurely pace, filtering the matter that makes its way down from the surface for food.

The Toxic Songbird

"Us? You want to feed *us* to your dog? Look, I respect the fact that you caught us—that's pretty impressive seeing as we have wings and you don't—but I'm telling you right now, this is a bad, *terrible* idea. If you want our advice—and you don't seem to because you're ignoring us, but regardless—feed us to some stray you picked up on the street. Someone's gonna die either way, that's for sure, and it just doesn't make sense that you'd want it to be your own pet. You know?"

IN THE EARLY 1800s, French-born ornithologist, naturalist, and painter John James Audubon was traveling along the Mississippi River when he decided to put the rumors of the Carolina parakeet's (*Conuropsis carolinensis*) toxicity to the test. Dash, his hunting dog, was to be the guinea pig.

Carolina parakeets were a species of small parrots, resplendent in jade green, pale yellow, and gold plumage, and they had once littered the southeastern United States. Rumored to be poison birds, they gained a reputation from the native Americans and settlers alike as having the capacity to kill a cat, as Audubon mentioned in a journal entry from December 29, 1820:

We Boiled ten Parokeets tonight for Dash who has had ten Welps—purposely to try . . . the Poisoning effect of their hearts on animals. Yesterday We Were told that seven Cats had been Killed Last Summer by Eating as Many Parokeets.

What happened to Dash following a meal of Carolina parakeets was never confirmed, but Audubon kept a very thorough journal, and following the previous entry, Dash was never mentioned again.

Just a few years earlier, Scottish-American poet and ornithologist Alexander Wilson decided to test the Carolina parakeet's poison on his pet as well—a cat called Mrs. Puss. But cats will be cats, and Mrs. Puss proved a far less doting guinea pig than poor old Dash, according to Wilson writing in *Wilson's American Ornithology* in 1808:

A very general opinion prevails, that the brains and intestines of the Carolina Parakeet are a sure and fatal poison to cats. I had determined, when at Big Bone, to put this to the test of experiment; and for that purpose collected the brains and bowels of more than a dozen of them. But after close search Mrs. Puss was not to be found, being engaged perhaps on more agreeable business.

Wilson convinced a friend to feed the poison birds to her cats instead, testing a mother cat and her two kittens himself, only to find all had lived after consuming every part, leaving just the beaks. Why these cats had not succumbed to the Carolina parakeet's poison was a mystery, but Wilson put it down to the difference in diet between the wild and captive birds. "Still, however, the effect might have been different, had the daily food of the bird been cockle burrs, instead of Indian corn," he wrote in *American Ornithology: Or the Natural History of the Birds of the United States*. The seeds of the cockle burr plant were a known poison to cats, so Wilson concluded that this could be the source of the Carolina parakeet's poisonous insides.

Now extinct due to deforestation and overhunting, the Carolina parakeet was worn down to a single captive male called Incas, who died in 1918. Yet a few species of toxic birds remain today, most notably in the New Guinea bush where, in 1989, chairman and assistant curator of the Department of Ornithology and Mammalogy at the California Academy of Sciences, Jack Dumbacher, stumbled on the extraordinary secret of a striking bird called the hooded pitohui. Dumbacher recalls his first encounter with the pitohui:

> It was all very accidental. I was in Papua New Guinea with a team of folks studying Raggiana birds of paradise. We had many mist nets scattered in the forest for catching the birds of paradise, but we caught many other birds as well. One day, several hooded pitohuis were in a net. These are large birds that can cut your hands, and as I struggled to free them, they bit and scratched my hands. These little scratches really stung, so I just put my fingers in my mouth to clean the cut, and after a minute or so my lips and tongue began to tingle and burn. After this happened to one of our volunteers, we put the stories together and wondered whether it was possible if the bird was the source of the tingling. The next time we caught a pitohui, we tasted a feather, and there was the tingling burning sensation—and the toxin. When we asked the local guides, they all seemed to know about this.

Popping a feather on his tongue, Dumbacher reported that the tingling sensation could last for hours, and gathered a bunch to take back with him to the States. Serendipitously, the chemist who agreed to identify the pitohui's poison was John Daly from the National Institutes of Health, the man who in the 1960s discovered batrachotoxins—extremely potent neurotoxic steroidal alkaloids— in the poison dart frogs of Central and South America. Ounce for ounce, this is one of the most toxic natural substances known, and in 1992, Daly isolated this same poison in a sample from one of Dumbacher's birds. That year the poisonous pitohui and Dumbacher's discovery found itself on the cover of *Science*.

In 2004, Dumbacher reported in *Proceedings of the National Academy of Sciences* that a group of New Guinea villagers had identified where the pitohuis sourced their batrachotoxins. Just as the Texas horned lizard gets its poison from *Pogonomyrmex* ants, it appeared as if a group of small, colorful beetles called melyrids were the origin of the hooded pitohui's poison. "We found the same toxins in these beetles, and we found the beetles in the birds' stomachs. These toxins would poison most other birds, so first you would have to evolve some resistance to the toxin yourself, and only afterward could it be of some use in defense," says Dumbacher, highlighting just how tricky it is in evolutionary terms for a bird to render itself toxic. Because when you can just fly away, why go to all the trouble of maintaining your toxicity?

PART FIVE

ODD BODIES

A (Mostly)
Vegetarian Spider

"Okay, let me make this easy for you, *Bagheera kiplingi.* Who here hasn't heard that you're a vegetarian now? Absolutely no one? This is exactly my point, *Bagheera kiplingi.*"

A WIDE-EYED JUMPING SPIDER from southeastern Mexico and northwestern Costa Rica called *Bagheera kiplingi* is the first known mostly vegetarian spider. Discovered in the late 1800s and named after Rudyard Kipling's *Jungle Book* panther, it wasn't until 2009 that researchers, publishing in *Current Biology,* identified the unique eating habits that set it apart from the 40,000 other species of spider in the world. Instead of consuming the liquefied remains of insect, lizard, bird, or small mammal prey like most spider species, *B.*

kiplingi prefers to eat whole plant material. (It does cheat, though, occasionally snacking on an ant, spider, or ant larvae.)

According to lead researcher and biologist Christopher Meehan from the University of Arizona, *B. kiplingi* is the first spider ever found to specifically "hunt" plants, treating them as a primary food source. "I've done the math several times, and even the most conservative estimates point to near-total vegetarianism."

While some orb-weaving spider species have been observed eating pollen on occasion, it's very rare to see a spider eat solid material such as leaves, particularly something like Beltian bodies. These detachable tips, found on some species of *Acacia* shrubs, are rich in lipids, proteins, and sugars, but are also 80 percent structural fiber, so are pretty bulky by a spider's standards. "Spiders aren't really thought to be capable of eating solid food at all," says Meehan.

B. kiplingi has learned to take advantage of a special mutual relationship between the wasplike *Pseudomyrmex* ants and *Acacia* plants in which the ants protect the plant from predators and the plant supplies them with nutrient-rich Beltian bodies. By building their nests in the oldest, most withered *Acacia* leaves where the *Pseudomyrmex* ants are unlikely to patrol, *B. kiplingi* will use careful evasion tactics and its hydraulically propelled jump to make its way to a Beltian body and back to its nest undetected. If spotted, it will use a line of silk to drop to safety. Meehan also speculated that it might even be able to mimic the ants' scent in order to mask its presence. "Jumping spiders in general possess incredibly advanced sensory-cognitive skills and eight-legged agility, and *Bagheera* is no exception," he said. "Individuals employ diverse, situation-specific strategies to evade ants, and the ants simply cannot catch them."

The Strangest Mammal in the World

NAKED MOLE RAT
(*Heterocephalus glaber*)

"You cannot hurt me, Mr. Bond. I am impervious to acid. I can't get cancer. I can live in the foulest, darkest, deepest cave you find. You cannot *touch* me, Mr. Bond!"

"When was the last time you had sex with a female?"

"Well played, Mr. Bond. Well played."

IT DOESN'T MATTER HOW well you think you know the naked mole rat, it will always end up being far weirder than you think. This is a cold-blooded, hairless, near-blind, bucktoothed rodent that can not only tolerate acid and chili heat, but can run backwards and resist cancer. Right down to their misshapen sperm and insectlike colonies, these might just be the strangest mammals on the planet.

Naked mole rats, otherwise known as sand puppies and saber-toothed sausages, are native to the harsh, drier areas of East Africa, including southern Ethiopia, Kenya, and Somalia. On average they grow to be about 4 inches long and 1 ounce in weight, and live almost 7 feet below the ground, densely packed into a complex system of pitch-black burrows. Here they happily breathe in oxygen-starved, carbon-dioxide–saturated air that would kill any other mammal; a naked mole rat tunnel has an atmospheric level of 10 percent carbon dioxide, while the normal atmospheric level of carbon dioxide is 0.04 percent.

Naked mole rats are one of just two species of mammals known to live in eusocial, or insectlike, colonies. Up to 300 naked mole rat individuals will live together in a colony, ruled over by a massive 3-ounce queen. Once she has literally shoved any contending females out the way, the queen will become the only female in the colony that can reproduce, selecting a single male as her mate. Most of the remaining "subordinate" males and all other females are reproductively suppressed for as long as the queen rules, but occasionally a subordinate male will father her offspring.

At the European Society of Human Reproduction and Embryology conference in 2007, Chris Faulkes from the School of Biological and Chemical Sciences at the University of London reported that the stress of the queen's dominating behavior appeared to block puberty in the rest of the females, keeping their reproductive tracts underdeveloped. But Faulkes discovered that this phenomenon can be reversed—when the queen dies, the highest ranked of the remaining females will fight it out to find the new queen, who will very quickly become reproductively active.

By restricting the reproductive competition among the entire colony to one female, and one to three males, naked mole rat sperm has evolved to become simple, strange, and sluggish. In 2011, researchers from South Africa examined the sperm from males of different social statuses and found that not only did the sperm look weird, with irregular-shaped heads, poorly developed necks, and the smallest midpiece (the area at the base of the sperm head) of any known mammal, a dismal 1–15 percent of them could actually swim, and a mere 1 percent could be considered "fast" swimmers.

By comparison, 70 percent of a dog's, 60 percent of a stallion's, and more than 50 percent of a human's sperm will be healthy and forward moving. Somehow, despite the appalling mobility and structure of the sperm, the researchers found that the naked mole rat males could father a number of healthy offspring each litter.

With the protection of her entire colony, the queen can afford to have exceptionally long gestation periods of 70 days—rats have gestation periods of 20–24 days—and produce the biggest litters of any mammal, with an average of 28 pups five times a year. And according to Paul W. Sherman from Cornell University in New York, they break all the rules when it comes to nursing. Mammals usually produce roughly half as many young in one litter as they have mammary glands, but naked mole rat mothers do the opposite. "Most mammals follow the one-half rule," says Sherman, who published in the *Journal of Mammalogy* in 1999. "That is, they produce about one half as many young in each litter as they have mammae. In general, females have enough mammae for each young in the largest litters to have his or her own. It even works for humans, where our average litter size is one, but twins sometimes occur."

Sherman and his colleagues suggested that the reason naked mole rats don't have twice as many mammaries as pups is that infections could spread more easily with a large number of mammary glands. And despite the competition for food, the pups don't seem to fight over the mammaries. They'll quietly wait their turn or be nursed by another female in the colony. "This is one more reason why *Heterocephalus glaber* are so interesting to biologists," says Sherman. "They live like social insects, the adults share food and defense tasks, they have the largest litters of any known mammal, they are closely related, and now, it appears, the young are willing to share mother's milk. These animals have evolved to break the rules, because of their extreme sociality."

They might not have a protective layer of fur or hair, and their skin isn't particularly thick, but the naked mole rat has an incredible resistance to pain in its skin. While they react to temperature and pressure in the same way that other rodents do, they have evolved to lack a chemical in their bodies called Substance P, which is a neurotransmitter associated with certain types of pain. When a typical mammal sustains an injury or a burn that produces a long-lasting ache, the pain fibers that signal to their central nervous system will release Substance P, provoking a pain sensation. In 2008, researchers from Chicago and Berlin inserted a modified herpes cold sore virus into naked mole rats to deliver the genes for Substance P to the nerve fibers in one of their feet. Upon restoring the rodents' sense of pain using this technique, the researchers tested their reaction to capsaicin, the active component in chilies, to all four feet. They found that only the foot with Substance P in its nerve fibers provoked a reaction.

Unexpectedly, the researchers, reporting in *PLoS Biology*, found that the Substance P–infused naked mole rats still showed no reaction when acid was applied to their skin. "The mole rat is the only animal that shows completely no response to acid," says coauthor Thomas Park from the University of Illinois.

Late last year, the German researchers investigated the naked mole rat's apparent insensitivity to acid. In most mammals' body tissues, carbon dioxide is converted into acid, which, when it builds up, continuously activates the body's pain sensors. Because this rodent lives in an environment where carbon dioxide levels are incredibly high, the research suggested that through evolution they have ended up with altered sodium ion channels in their pain receptors that are inactivated by any kind of acid. There are rare cases of humans born without these types of ion channels, called Nav1.7, who cannot feel pain, and there's a type of local anesthetic that dentists use that has sodium ion channel blockers to induce this same insensitivity to pain.

Around the same time, researchers from the University of Liverpool's Institute of Integrative Biology in England sequenced the complete genome of the naked mole rat to figure out how it can live for up to three decades in harsh underground conditions—while avoiding cancer the entire time—while other rodents such as mice can only manage a lifespan of four years. Working with scientists from Harvard University, the team discovered that particular genes of the naked mole rat that are associated with mitochondria—tiny organelles that provide the energy a cell requires to move and divide—and respiratory and cell decision-making systems are expressed in abnormally high levels when compared to the same genes in regular wild mice. The researchers, publishing in *PLoS ONE* in late 2011, suggested that high levels of genes associated with energy production and cell decision-making processes may be the key to the animal's anti-aging, anti-cancer intracellular environment.

For all their truly bizarre qualities, some scientists are pushing for the naked mole rat to become more widely used in scientific research, replacing the grossly overused and farmed common mouse. If they can teach us how they have managed to completely avoid contracting cancer, even when tumors are deliberately implanted inside their bodies to see if they will grow, that would really be something.

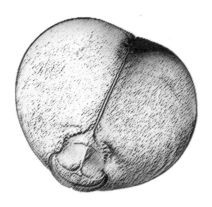

Flying Buttocks

ALMOST 3280 FEET BELOW the ocean surface, the pigbutt worm doesn't do much besides float around looking like the rear end of a pig. Named *Chaetopterus pugaporcinus*—which literally means "worm that looks like a pig's rump"—the pigbutt worm was discovered in 2006 by Monterey Bay Aquarium Research Institute's Karen Osborn (of swima worm fame). It was scooped up by a remotely operated vehicle (ROV) patrolling the mesopelagic zone just off Monterey Bay in California, which occupies the ocean from 656 feet below the surface to around 3280 feet. While a little sunlight penetrates it through the epipelagic zone directly above, many animals in the mesopelagic rely on bioluminescence for signaling and communication.

You only have to look at this otherworldly blue balloon with its pink, puckered mouth to know that this is unlike any other worm in the world. Osborn found that although it has a segmented body, one of the middle segments is flat, causing the two outer segments to inflate like a balloon to give it the appearance of a rear end. Because it shares some similarities with the larvae of a group of marine filter feeding polychaete (or segmented) worms called the Chaetopteridae, Osborn thought the pigbutt worm might be in its larval stage. However, it being the relatively formidable size (for a marine worm) of a hazelnut, Osborn conceded in a 2007 issue of the *Biological Bulletin*, "If the specimens described here are larvae, they are remarkable for their size, which . . . is five to ten times larger than any known chaetopterid larvae."

The only other option was that this worm was in its adult form, making it the strangest-looking adult chaetopterid anyone had ever seen. All known adult chaetopterid worms have long, segmented bodies, and live inside vertical or horseshoe-shaped tubes inside tunnels buried in the seafloor. Here they spend their days catching plankton with the mucus net they make and suspend over the top of the tube. But the pigbutt worm drifts at a depth of 2950–3935 feet, its downward-turned mouth surrounded by a cloud of mucus, which Osborn thinks might be used to capture tiny food particles and detritus that float down from the higher water levels. The pig-butt worms also lack reproductive organs, which makes them even more inscrutable, but Osborn says that this means the specimens that were caught were not immediately in the process of reproducing, not that they don't do so. "Many annelid [segmented] worms only have evidence of reproductive organs when actively reproducing, which can be for just a few weeks to a couple months," she added.

Unable to classify this worm based on morphological features, Osborn and her team analyzed the DNA from dozens of marine worms, creating the first family tree to represent the relationships between twelve species of chaetopterid worms. This didn't help them discover whether this new species is in its larval or adult form, but the team suggested that its strange appearance may be the result of the larvae finding themselves unable to settle on the seafloor like the other worms, which hindered the growth process, restricting them to the larval form forever. "They may be larvae that missed their cue to settle out to the seafloor or never found suitable habitat, but that seems unlikely considering the consistency with which we find them in a specific midwater habitat and the consistency of their morphology no matter what size they are (ranging from 0.5–1 inch)," says Osborn. "They always have the same number of segments and the same mix of larval and adult characters. It would be nice to find one in the process of reproducing so we would know if they can complete their life cycle wholly within the water column."

Yeah, so the pigbutt worm might look like the rear end of a disgusting mammal, but that doesn't seem to bother him. Cruising around, not giving a shit about what the other chaetopterid worms are doing is what made him a pigbutt worm in the first place, so I bet they're generally pretty chill. Like, it'd be the first day of high school and Pigbutt Worm will be transferring from another school and all the cool kids will be like, "OMG. Have you seen the new guy? He looks like ass," while they hang out in their tubes on the seafloor.

And Pigbutt Worm will float past, pretty much oblivious but also not really caring, being all, "Hey man, what's up?"

And most of the cool kids will continue to make fun of him, blaming their farts on him and making him do chemistry pracs on his own, but Pigbutt Worm will take it all in his stride, and after school will hang out with the more mature college kids who don't give a shit about things just as hard as he doesn't give a shit about things. Of course, this will invariably lead to one of the cool females hatching a scheme with one of the cool males to set Pigbutt Worm up with the cool female's older sister so her overbearing dad will let them both go to the school dance, and that's good for the cool male because he'll get to bang the cool female after the dance for the first time. And Pigbutt Worm will go along with it because he doesn't really give a shit and was probably high the whole time anyway.

But as things progress, Pigbutt Worm will develop an actual crush on the sister because she almost doesn't give a shit harder than he doesn't give a shit, and she'll start to like him back because she hates most people except for him. Of course, the scheme will be revealed at the dance, when everyone is dressed up in their suits and evening gowns made of seaweed, and the sister will think Pigbutt Worm doesn't give a shit about anything, especially her, even though he does.

And then a huge fish will crash through the upturned shell that is the dance hall and swallow everyone in a single gulp. Guess that overbearing dad was right after all.

The Elusive Stick Giant

"Jehovah's Witnesses? Seriously? How the fuck did you guys find me out here?"

FOR AN INSECT TO be otherwise known as a "land lobster," you know it's got to be seriously big. The Lord Howe Island stick insect is a flightless, nocturnal insect that stretches up to 5 inches long, its solid, rust-colored body weighing around 0.28–0.32 ounces. When you consider the average cockroach doesn't grow beyond one tenth of an ounce, you can get a pretty good idea of how large these things are. But the enormous size of the Lord Howe Island stick insect, which gives them an air of something prehistoric, is not the strangest thing about them. In 2001, these hefty stick insects were brought back from the dead.

Lord Howe Island is a crescent-shaped volcanic island that sits between Australia and New Zealand about 373 miles from Port Macquarie in New South Wales, with a population of around 350 people. In the nineteenth century the Lord Howe Island stick insect prowled this Australian territory in such numbers that fishermen would use them as bait and ladies would dread finding them in their outhouse toilets. But then the rodents came. Mice were introduced to the island in the 1880s, followed by black rats in 1918 when they hitched a ride on the British vessel *SS Makambo*, and they made more than a meal or two out of the island's meaty insect residents, not to mention its unique species of birds. Sightings of the Lord Howe Island stick insect dropped off dramatically shortly afterwards, until by 1920 not a single one was recorded, and by 1960 they were officially proclaimed extinct.

But in the late 1960s, sightings of stick insect remains were reported on Ball's Pyramid, a supersheer volcanic remnant that sits 12 miles from Lord Howe Island. Said to be the tallest volcanic stack in the world, Ball's Pyramid is about 1805 feet high, around 985 feet wide and 0.6 miles long, and it's so narrow that there's no way anyone's landing a boat on it. Instead, you have to anchor your boat in the ocean surrounding it, launch yourself onto the vertical pyramid wall and climb your way up. Needless to say, this place is an explorer's dream, and many climbing groups were desperate to seek out the fabled stick insect. But in 1984, the Lord Howe Island Board, a seven-member group sanctioned by the NSW government to handle environmental concerns regarding the territory, banned any climbing on Ball's Pyramid except for scientific work. And even then, you would have to make a really impressive case to gain approval.

Between 1998 and 2001, Australian scientists David Priddel and Nicholas Carlile began planning their way onto Ball's Pyramid— not to find the Lord Howe Island stick insect, but to prove, once and for all, that the species was dead and gone. The pair, who worked for the NSW Government's Office of Environment and Heritage on issues related to the recovery of threatened species, knew they couldn't just grab any scientist and get climbing approval, so they recruited local ranger Dean Hiscox, entomologist Stephen Fellenberg, and entomology curator Margaret Humphrey from the Macleay Museum at the University of Sydney. "David and I decided the only way to mount a trip to Ball's

Pyramid was to take some entomologists, and to prove the things weren't there," says Carlile.

It took four years for the team to make it out to Lord Howe Island, and even once they got there in 2001, they had wait for almost a week for just the right sea conditions before attempting to cross over and land on Ball's Pyramid. There's no way you'd attempt to launch yourself onto the sheer wall of Ball's Pyramid from a tiny boat in choppy waters. The researchers also knew that the Lord Howe Island stick insect was nocturnal, so rather than attempting to look for the animals themselves, which meant climbing the formation at night, they decided to look for droppings or any other indications of the insect during the day. "We knew from stories passed down from the locals, and the one scientific paper [published in 1969 by Australian entomologist Arthur Mills Lea], that they are nocturnal, and lived inside logs and hollows in trees because they couldn't cope with drying out in the Sun," says Carlile.

Having established a base camp on a high wave-cut platform, they climbed about 490 feet up the side of Ball's Pyramid to Gannet Green, with the largest invertebrate find being remains of a couple of large crickets. The harsh conditions forced them back to their base before day's end, so before getting dizzy and dehydrated, they edged their way back down to the boat. On their way down, the researchers noticed a group of *Melaleuca howeana* bushes growing from within a small crevice that seeped water, supported by a peaty buildup of soil—possibly the only place like it containing what could be the only patch of soil on the whole of Ball's Pyramid. *M. howeana* is a dense, short bush endemic to Lord Howe Island, and is hardy enough to thrive in exposed, rocky sites. Underneath this one bush was, as Carlile described it, "several large insect frass (poos)."

The researchers thought it was likely that the sizeable poo belonged to one of the large crickets they had seen earlier that day, but the only way to prove it was from the Lord Howe Island stick insect was to return to the *Melaleuca* bush that night. "We had an instamatic camera (it was predigital days) with three shots left, and a head torch each. I hadn't had my kids at that stage so I was still up for a bit of derring-do," says Carlile. "We found the shrub and there were two bloody huge insects straddling it." At that point, the researchers became the only people alive to have ever seen a living Lord Howe Island stick insect. "It was just phenomenal. Even twelve, thirteen years later it is one of the highlights of my life. We'd been talking about and planning this trip for years because we wanted to show that it wasn't there, so this total 180 was surprising to say the least," says Carlile.

Looking inside the *Melaleuca*, they found a juvenile stick insect. Incredibly, it turned out that this one bush sustained the entire Ball's Pyramid population of Lord Howe Island stick insects—between twenty-four and forty individuals—which meant it sustained the entire species. Stick insects are generally pretty flexible when it comes to eating different types of plants, so long as they are introduced to it as juveniles, but what they can't live without is soil because their eggs won't hatch on dry, spare rock. "This single shrub is significant to the entire species of the invertebrate. That's why it is so rare," says Carlile. For this reason the Lord Howe Island stick insect gained the reputation of being the rarest insect on Earth. Just how they made it from Lord Howe Island to the safety of the rodentless Ball's Pyramid, when they couldn't fly, is something no one has been able to answer conclusively, but Carlile thinks they were either tossed onto the rocks as discarded fish bait, or were mistakenly collected as nesting material by a type of seabird called the Common Noddy.

In 2003, the researchers were given approval to collect two breeding pairs of Lord Howe Island stick insects. They gave one to Fellenberg to breed in Sydney and one to the Melbourne Zoo. Fellenberg's female died, as they can be a tricky species to keep in captivity, but from the Melbourne Zoo pair, 21 eggs were produced from which healthy young hatched. According to Carlile, the Zoo now has about 1000 adults and 20,000 eggs. The plan now is to go back to Ball's Pyramid and collect more eggs to improve the genetic robustness of the captive population, but, as with the researchers' first trip out there in 2001, this requires a lot of planning, and waiting for the perfect conditions. "The window just hasn't been there," says Carlile. The long-term plan for these rediscovered insects is for the rats and mice to be completely eradicated from Lord Howe Island as early as 2015—a $10 million project, according to Carlile—and the captive population reintroduced with a species of owl to keep them in check. "We can't reintroduce them now," says Carlile, "But that is our aim."

At Home in Someone Else's Anus

THIS SLENDER, TRANSLUCENT, AND scaleless fish really takes advantage of being pencil thin. Not content to make its own home in the seabed or the crevices of rocks, almost all species of the pearlfish family live in the body cavities of invertebrates such as clams, oysters, and starfish. And a notorious few reside exclusively in the anuses of sea cucumbers.

"Pearlfish" is the common name of the Carapidae family, which includes thirty-one species of fish that live in the tropical waters of every ocean on Earth except the Arctic, and can be found in both shallow waters and at a depth of up to 1.2 miles below the surface. The family earned its common name after a dead pearlfish was discovered inside an oyster shell; it had been encrusted and paralyzed by the substance produced by an oyster to create its shell's second inner layer—the mother-of-pearl lining.

Not all pearlfish find the experience of residing inside other sea creatures so perilous. On the contrary, this behavior ensures a safe haven for the delicate fish, keeping them hidden from predators during the day, before a spot of nocturnal foraging, according to some researchers. Some species find sea cucumbers (*Holothuriidae*) to be particularly accommodating hosts, as they are found in great numbers in the world's oceans, often forming very dense populations in shallower waters, plus they move sluggishly and are extremely nonaggressive scavengers. So genial are sea cucumbers that of all the echinoderms—a large group of "spiny-skinned" marine animals including starfish and sea urchins—they are the most heavily parasitized, playing host to a menagerie of smaller creatures such as crabs, worms, and bacteria.

Once a pearlfish species from the *Carapus* or *Encheliophis* genera stumbles across a sea cucumber, it will locate its new host's anus, or cloaca, by following the current of water that is inhaled and expelled out of it via a structure called the respiratory tree. Sea cucumbers are the only animals in the world to have respiratory trees and they are one of three sites, along with the tube feet and body wall, by which the creatures take in oxygen from the water. With the anus located, the pearlfish—which can grow up to 20 inches long—will tap the anus area a little before penetrating the sea cucumber by one of two methods: headfirst, propelling itself inside by violently thrusting its tail from side to side, or tail first, coordinating its inwards slide with the sea cucumber's next exhale. Once inside, the pearlfish settles into the respiratory tree.

Now you know why the pearlfish is otherwise known as the assfish. They are also built to be an assfish, their anuses set in a position on the body that allows them to emerge partway out of the host to excrete waste into the ocean without having to completely exit and risk predation.

Most often, pearlfish don't like to share their hosts with other pearlfish; however, there have been cases of some *Encheliophis* species living in sexual pairs inside their sea cucumbers. And in 1977, New Zealand biologist Victor Benno Meyer-Rochow from Jacobs University in Germany discovered a 16-inch-long sea cucumber into which no less than fifteen pearlfish had taken up residence.

While researchers are yet to prove whether or not sea cucumbers act as a breeding site for the pearlfish, they do provide an environment in which their larvae can transform into their adult forms, which sees their eel-like bodies thicken and then shorten by up to 60 percent.

While the sea cucumber–pearlfish relationship has been well known for many years, how the pearlfish behaved toward one another when competing for a host was not clearly understood. In 2002, scientists from the University of California in Santa Cruz decided to find out. They examined two species of sea cucumber hosts: a black-skinned species called the pineapple sea cucumber (*Thelenota ananas*), which wears a coat of fleshy projections called papillae in the shape of sunset orange–colored stars; and the leopard sea cucumber (*Bohadschia argus*), a portly golden or grey sausage of an animal with a psychedelic splattering of dirty white haloes across its leathery skin. The leopard sea cucumber grows up to 20 inches long and the pineapple sea cucumber can stretch to a little over 3 feet.

Collecting a number of each sea cucumber species from their natural habitats, the team observed the relationships between the pearlfish and the sea cucumbers in the lab. They found that the pearlfish would fight to the death over a host—sometimes *inside* a host—and would actively check if anyone was home before entering. "Both species of carapids seemed to listen along the body of the host almost as if trying to detect the presence of another occupant inside," the team reported.

Gross, Pearlfish. Just . . . I'm trying to find a redeeming feature but what do you say about an assfish? You'd better have a cool job or something because that's honestly the only way you're going to get anyone to talk to you. Stop laughing, I'm trying to help you! Okay, say you meet someone: a girl, a prospective boss, a friend of a friend of a friend at a party, it doesn't matter, Pearlfish. Here's how I see your opening conversation going.

Scenario 1

> "Hi, I'm Robin."
>
> "Hi, I'm Pearlfish."
>
> "That's a pretty name. Where do you live?"
>
> "In an anus."
>
> "Oh my God. What do you do?"
>
> "I'm a poet."
>
> "Hey, that's cool."

Scenario 2

> "Hi, I'm Robin."
>
> "Hi, I'm Pearlfish."
>
> "That's a pretty name. Where do you live?"
>
> "In an anus."
>
> "Oh my god. What do you do?"
>
> "I'm an artist."
>
> "Hey, that's cool."

Scenario 3

> "Hi, I'm Robin."
>
> "Hi, I'm Pearlfish."
>
> "That's a pretty name. Where do you live?"
>
> "In an anus."
>
> "Oh my god. What do you do?"
>
> "I'm a judge on *MasterChef*."

"The nice one?"

"We're *all* nice. That's the point."

"Yeah, true. Hey, that's cool."

Scenario 4

"Hi, I'm Robin."

"Hi, I'm Pearlfish."

"That's a pretty name. Where do you live?"

"In an anus."

"Oh my god. What do you do?"

"Nothing/Banker/Waiter/Mechanic." (It doesn't matter at this point, Pearlfish.)

"That's so fucked."

Houdini with an Inflatable Head

"Mr. C. indagator, I'm sorry to tell you, but your wife has decided she wants half of all your assets. You didn't sign a prenup; you slept with a Mexican stripper. Twice. There's just no escaping this."

"Oh yeah?" *pfft pfft pfft* "How about now?"

"You're still ruined, *Mr. C. indagator.* And now your head isn't going to fit through the door."

WHEN YOU NEED TO get out of a tight spot, ordinarily you'd be advised to think small. Unless you're a *Cacoxenus indagator*, in which case you've got to think big.

C. indagator is a species of fly that lives in Western Europe, with ruby red eyes bulging out of a dusty black body. It belongs to the Drosophilidae family of flies, which is a large, diverse group that includes the well-known common fruit fly (*Drosophila melanogaster*). And just like the fruit fly, *C. indagator* has a particular penchant for sweet substances and has evolved an extraordinary mechanism for acquiring them as larvae.

The object of *C. indagator*'s desire is the pollen and nectar mixture that the red mason bee (*Osmia bicornis*) stores in its tube-shaped nest. The red mason bee, which is a fuzzy black and copper-colored species from all over Europe, North America,

Turkey, and Iran, is what's known as a solitary bee. This means that rather than living in a nest built by the entire colony, as honeybees do, the red mason bee will move into any thin tunnels or cavities they come across, whether holes burrowed into a tree trunk by a beetle or cracks in crumbling masonry around populated areas. Every spring, the female red mason bee drops her mixture of pollen and nectar into the farthest end of the tube, attaches a single egg to the wall, and closes the two of them in by constructing a 0.08–0.24-inch-thick wall of mud that quickly dries hard. She will repeat the process all the way up the tube nest, filling each brood cavity with an egg and a package of sweet nutrients.

Over the following months, the egg will hatch into a larva that will spin itself into a cocoon when old enough, and eventually emerge as an adult. At this point it will have mandibles strong enough to nibble its way through its mother's mud wall, which it will do to release itself from the tube nest. Of course, a package of nutrients is the perfect food resource for a parasitic species, but many do not have mandibles strong enough to break their way through the mud walls, such as the flies that raid dauber wasp cavities—around 12 percent won't make it out alive. But *C. indagator* has figured out a way around this, as Erhard Strohm, an entomologist from the Institute of Zoology at Germany's University of Regensburg, discovered in late 2010.

"We observed *Cacoxenus* that were freshly enclosed from their cocoons for a project with the aim to analyze how they orientate to emerge from the brood cells of their hosts and we had the working hypothesis that the flies use the same cues as the bees themselves," says Strohm.

Under a stereomicroscope, I saw that the young flies touched the walls with their forelegs, probably in order to detect the side that is convex, since this is the side that points to the entrance of the nest. Surprisingly, they then started to press their heads into small crevices at this side of the nest partition and their head blisters began to pulse and were eventually fully inflated.

So *C. indagator* hides itself inside a brood cell, eats another species' offspring and then inflates it own head to break itself free. But how does one inflate one's own head without damaging oneself? By filming them, Strohm was able to figure out that they pump hemolymph, which is the fluid in the circulatory system of some arthropods that acts like blood, into their ptilinum—a pouch on the head above the base of the antenna that can be turned outward or inside out. Publishing in *Physiological Entomology*, Strohm described the closed-in fly as being able to locate small crevices in the mud walls, against which it would press its body and abruptly expand its head, breaking pieces of the partition away using hydraulic pressure.

This process would only take from 5–30 seconds, and because the fly is still young at this stage, it is able to squeeze its soft, developing body through the small hole it has created and escape. "Interestingly, the cuticle is still very soft, so that they can 'distort' their bodies to a large extent. I actually do not know whether *C. indagator* can inflate their head blisters more than when breaking down the walls of their cocoons," says Strohm. He found that if multiple flies are trapped in a brood cell together, they will work in the same area to create a single exit hole. About a third of the flies observed in the study escaped by inflating their heads, the rest waited for the mother red mason bee to return and unwittingly break them out.

C. indagator presents a huge problem for the red mason bee, in some cases parasitizing more than 40 percent of its brood cells. And according to Strohm, in most cases the bee larvae will die from starvation in the cell. "In most places *Cacoxenus* is by far the most important parasite of *Osmia bicornis*," he says. But it's not like the bees haven't figured out what's going on, he said, adding:

> I once observed a nest where a Cacoxenus was actually beginning to oviposit [lay eggs] into a brood cell when the female unexpectedly returned. The Cacoxenus immediately "understood" and quickly ran towards the entrance of the nest, thus passing the incoming female in the nest tube. The female startled and appeared to search for an intruder and it seemed to check the brood cell (possibly for eggs). I had thought that the Cacoxenus had left the nest, however, the stupid fly returned, the bee turned around then the fly also turned around and tried to escape. The bee was faster, and it grasped the fly with its comparatively large mandibles and within a second, chewed it and then threw it out of the nest.

The Toughest Fish in Outer Space

AT NO MORE THAN 6 inches long, the blunt-nosed, stout-bodied killifish is about as unassuming as a fish can get. But don't be fooled—this could well be the toughest fish on Earth.

Found off the coast of North America and in the Gulf of St. Lawrence—the world's largest estuary, encapsulated by the coasts of Newfoundland, Quebec, Nova Scotia, and New Brunswick in Canada—the killifish is famous for its ability to live in a range of water salinities, ranging from fresh to heavily salty water. There are a number of species, known as euryhaline organisms, which carry this ability, such as the bull shark, the herring, the puffer fish, and the barramundi, but none can compete with the killifish's tremendous level of adaptability. They can live quite happily in any muddy pool, creek, or ditch, any salty marsh, polluted harbor, or brackish estuary you throw at them; they are unfazed by a severe lack of oxygen, high levels of carbon dioxide, or foul substances in their water, and even if their habitat dries up completely, they can survive in the surrounding mud, flopping overland until they reach the nearest body of water.

How this little fish can survive the kinds of environments that would kill just about any other species is what biologist Andrew Whitehead from Louisiana State University in Baton Rouge set out to discover, publishing his findings in mid-2010. "In Louisiana, these fish are well known among fishermen, who often use them for live bait," says Whitehead. "When curious Louisiana fishermen see me knocking around in marshes . . . I tell them that the reason I study them is that I'm interested in the evolution of physical toughness. Then they instantly get it, and usually launch into a series of stories often having to do with some extraordinary survival tale of killifish."

Whitehead collected six fish from the coastal waters of New Hampshire and kept them for three months in artificial seawater with a salinity level of 32 parts per thousand (ppt). The average level for ocean water is between 32 and 37 ppt. They were then transferred to freshwater and were tested for their bodies' reactions to the change in environment after 6, 24, 72, 168, and 336 hours at a time. Whitehead found the killifish to be extremely resilient, exhibiting changes in their blood plasma sodium levels at the 24-hour mark, but this was balanced out again by the 72-hour mark. "This is what I find most impressive of killifish, in that they can adjust their physiology and gill morphology to enable tolerance to freshwater all the way up to four times the salinity of seawater," says Whitehead. "The salt starts falling out of solution before you can kill them. If there were an Olympic event for osmotic tolerance, killifish would stand (swim?) alone on the podium."

When there is a sudden change in the solute concentration around an organism's cell, caused by high concentrations of salts, for example, water is drawn out of the cell in a process called osmosis which can severely damage the cell. Alternatively, if a cell is suddenly exposed to low concentrations of salts, an increased amount of water will enter the cell, causing it to swell and sometimes burst. Ordinarily, if you suddenly transport fish acclimatized to salt water to fresh water, they will likely experience osmotic shock, and if too many of their gill cells burst they will suffocate. The secret to the killifish's extreme osmotic tolerance, according to Whitehead's research, is that they are able to change the entire morphology of their gill structure to either retain ions in their blood when they end up in fresh water, or to actively pump out ions when in sea water to regulate the amount of water in their cells. This involves a dramatic transformation of the gill tissues and, according to Whitehead, certain populations of killifish can achieve this in a single day.

Whitehead puts the killifish's physiological flexibility down to the way it has adapted to its natural habitat—the estuary. Estuaries are shallow, partly enclosed coastal bodies of water that have freshwater rivers flowing into them, so their residents need to be able to cope with wild fluctuations of salinity, oxygen availability, temperature, and nutrient availabilities. These fluctuations can occur periodically with the tides or seasons, or randomly, such as when a storm hits, which will decrease the salinity of the water. "Estuaries are among the most dynamic habitats on the planet and impose severe physiological challenges on resident species," says Whitehead, who published his team's findings in the *Journal of Heredity*.

Also characteristic to the killifish is its ability to thrive in foul water that would kill any other fish, and the nature of this changes across individual populations, depending on what chemicals they are exposed to in their environment. Whitehead and his team examined three populations to discover their different survival mechanisms. One group lives in Newark Bay, an estuary in New Jersey where one of the biggest container shipping facilities in the United States, the Port Newark–Elizabeth Marine Terminal, is situated. The second population lives in New Bedford Harbor in

Massachusetts, and the third is in the Elizabeth River in Virginia. All three environments contain different levels of highly toxic, manmade carcinogenic chemicals, heavy metals, and pesticides, which make the water extremely difficult to live in.

The researchers compared the genetic make-up of these three populations of killifish to populations from clean estuaries. The New Bedford Harbor comparison found 16 percent of the genes were significantly different from the clean reference sites, the Newark Bay comparison found 32 percent of genes were different, and the Elizabeth River comparison found 8 percent of total genes were different. Further, they found very little overlap in the gene sets of the three populations, suggesting that the different chemical pollutants they grow up around brought about different evolutionary solutions.

Not only can this tough little fish survive in conditions on Earth that no other fish can, they can also survive in outer space. In 1973, a number of young killifish and their eggs were carried on NASA's *Skylab 3*, making them the very first fish in space. The astronauts conducted experiments to see how they coped in a zero-gravity environment and found that they were able to acclimate to weightlessness. In the first few days, they struggled to orient themselves, swimming in strange, circular patterns, but soon they got used to the change in environment and began to show less odd swimming behaviors by orienting their backs to the light source. "On Earth, fish can orient by using both gravity and light cues, which are normally in unison. In space, the gravity cue is of course removed, and it took a few days for the fish to cue into the remaining stimulus—light—to properly orient themselves," says Whitehead. While the killifish showed an extraordinary ability to adjust to a zero-gravity environment, the fish that were exposed to it at a young age exhibited permanent behavioral effects.

"This is fucking miserable, this is," declared Zden Lowy, the cook aboard the *Starship Compromise*. "We've been going around in circles for days and I'm this close to running out of potatoes."

"How close?" said Rout Hadley, a suave television broadcaster who was to announce whatever cosmic discoveries the crew made to the people back home. He was the only crew member who could stand talking to the wretched cook, but this was purely because he was a hypernarcissist who needed everyone he ever met to love and admire him and tell everyone they knew as much. "I wasn't looking."

"*This* close," repeated Lowy, somewhat impotently, because he hadn't actually gestured any kind of discernable quantity the first time, and certainly wasn't quick-witted enough to measure a space between his fins that he thought adequately signified how close they were to never having sausages and mashed potatoes again on command. So he just said "*This* close" in the hopes of Hadley understanding what he meant.

"Oh. Then what are you complaining about?" said Hadley, because he didn't.

The four-strong killifish crew of the *Starship Compromise* had been tasked by the astrobiologists at NASA to fly to Enceladus—Saturn's enigmatic moon—and investigate the possibility of life there. They had lost contact with the NASA astrobiologists about six months ago, to which the NASA astrobiologists responded with moderate levels of disappointment before moving on to their next project. The *Starship Compromise* crew responded with varying levels of panic, depending on their capacity to comprehend just how screwed they all were.

Hadley's level of panic was indifference. Nothing bad would ever happen to someone this good-looking, he reasoned, even if he was stuck in a spaceship that had been circling the same unidentified rocky planet for months because Captain Bsdot had utterly lost his nerve. "At least when we *do* run out of fuel, we'll have somewhere to land," he said before hitting the autopilot switch so he could work his way through the ship's liquor supply.

"Say, Lowy," said Hadley, "would you mind offering your opinion on how I look in a number of suits? I'm polling the crew to see which would be the best for when we first go to air."

"Sure, whatever," said Lowy, just as Captain Bsdot announced over the intercom that they had run out of fuel so were preparing to land on the unidentified rocky planet, where they would all surely die.

"Ssssshtrap yourselves in!" he added, before almost killing everyone with a landing that flipped the *Starship Compromise* around 180 degrees and then back again.

The sparse, rocky planet that constituted their new home was shaped roughly like a muffin, and was littered with great, dark boulders that made for very convincing chocolate chips. Ashen Peech, the resident engineer and the only female that Hadley hadn't successfully wooed in his entire life, shoved her space helmet on and opened the ship's hatch. "What the hell?"

A crowd of two, maybe three hundred aliens were staring up at Peech, blinking silently, waiting for her to utter the first means of communication between them. "Ahem!" yelled Peech, straining to reach the creatures right at the back, in case any of them were important. "Do you have any rocket fuel?" she continued, "and a GPS that can direct us back to Earth?"

The aliens, who could only be described as a bunch of raisins with eyes, blinked, and then a relatively large one in the front row stretched the skin where its mouth should be so tight that it broke apart and formed a mouth. "Are you fish?" it yelled back at the *Starship Compromise* crew.

"Yesh!" Captain Bsdot decided it was time he took charge of the situation, even if he did feel awfully queasy.

"We haven't had fish in a very long time," said the ralsin, to which the crew did not know how to respond, but then agreed when the raisin asked if they would like to be dinner.

"Have. I think you mean *have*," Hadley corrected them, having just emerged from his quarters in his tuxedo.

"Follow us," said the head raisin, before letting his mouth grow over into a wonky scar that looked almost like a grin.

"Well I guess things could be worse," said Captain Bsdot, taking a swig from his hipflask as he floated aimlessly through the blackness of space. "We could have been dinner."

"I wish we *were* dinner!" said Peech, struggling to stop herself from revolving head over tailfin. "If only Hadley hadn't tasted so horrible because of that disgusting pond he used to live in on Earth, we'd be out of our misery by now. We were *this* close!"

"How close?" said Captain Bsdot.

"This!" But Captain Bsdot had floated too far away to hear her.

Sunken Spider's Bubble Web

DIVING BELL SPIDER
(*Argyroneta aquatica*)

THE DIVING BELL IS a large device within which a diver can submerge him- or herself underwater and survive off the oxygen trapped inside. It was the earliest form of diving chamber ever invented, based on Aristotle's descriptions of a "cauldron that retains air" from the fourth century B.C., and was used and improved upon right up until the end of the seventeenth century. But a tiny creature has been using its own version of the diving bell for a whole lot longer than we have, and this one can sustain its occupant underwater for an entire day.

The diving bell spider is a remarkable species of air-breathing spider that spends virtually its entire life submerged underwater. It is found in freshwater ponds and lakes in northern and central Europe and parts of northern Asia, and is a good swimmer, capable of diving up to 98 feet below the surface. Not only is this species the only spider in the world to live its life under water, is it also one of the very few in which the males are bigger than the females, growing up to 0.7 inches and 0.5 inches long respectively.

The key to their unusual lifestyle is the net of silk they construct between submerged vegetation, which they then inflate with air bubbles trapped among the fine hairs covering their legs and abdomen. It only takes the diving bell spiders a few trips to the surface to collect enough bubbles to pump its "diving bell" so full of air that it can fit its body inside and sustain itself for hours. The size of the diving bell can range from small—just big enough for the spider to fit its abdomen inside—to large—allowing the spider to move its whole body in and out through the opening at the bottom. The shimmering, silvery appearance of the underwater web is where the name of the diving bell spider's genus, *Argyroneta*, comes from, meaning "silver net in the water" in Greek. The diving bell becomes the spider's home, where it remains for its entire life, laying its cocoon of eggs and hunting tiny aquatic insects and fish from within. But just how the diving bell spider breathes so effectively inside for such an extended period of time was, until very recently, a mystery.

Biologists Roger Seymour from the University of Adelaide in South Australia and Stefan Hetz from Berlin's Humboldt University decided to investigate. The pair collected some diving bell spiders from the wild with some difficulty, as this species is becoming increasingly rare in Europe, finally finding some in the Eider River in Germany. They recreated the conditions of a stagnant, weedy pond in the lab for the spiders, and after watching their spiders create their diving bells, they used an oxygen-measuring device called an optode to poke inside.

By taking a number of oxygen measurements inside the diving bell and surrounding water, Seymour and Hetz were able to calculate how much oxygen was flowing into each diving bell bubble and how much oxygen each spider was consuming. Publishing in the *Journal of Experimental Biology* in mid-2011, they reported that the underwater bubble could continuously exchange gases with the surrounding water, acting like a gill to provide the spiders with more oxygen from the water than was originally placed inside via the trapped air bubbles. The diving bell was so effective at being a gill that it could extract enough oxygen from the warm, stagnant water created by the researchers to sustain the spiders.

However, as nitrogen diffuses back into the surrounding water as a part of this process, the diving bell shrinks and must have its oxygen physically replenished. Seymour and Hetz discovered that despite previous studies stating that the diving bell spiders must return to the surface as often as every twenty minutes to renew the oxygen in the bubble, their spiders could remain submerged in their bubble for more than a day. Not only is this advantageous for the spiders, as frequently leaving their diving bell is likely to attract predators, but it shows just how effectively their bodies are able to metabolize the captured oxygen.

Spiders' Club Meeting 4/2

Present: *Evarcha culicivora*, Palpimanus Spider, *Bagheera kiplingi*, black-lace weaver spiderlings, Diving Bell Spider.

Housekeeping

Palpimanus Spider addresses buildup of broken chairs. Moves black-lace weaver spiderlings be charged due to excessive rocking. Vote: 4:1. Spiderlings to replace one chair per week. *Bagheera kiplingi* raises issue of club picnic food. Feels there aren't enough vegetarian options. *Evarcha culicivora* says there should be more blood if additional budget is allocated to vegetarian options. Palpimanus Spider feels more edible spiders should be added to picnic budget if more blood and vegetarian options are added. Discussion. Diving Bell Spider moves to keep picnic food as is due to competing interests. Unanimous vote. Diving Bell Spider moves to have pool installed in clubhouse. Vote: 1:4.

Birthdays

Nil

Projects

Diving Bell Spider says underwater tours still very unpopular. Requests funds for ten sets of scuba gear. Discussion. Request denied. *Evarcha culicivora* reports malaria project progress is slow, but steady.

Xmas Party

Bagheera kiplingi to check on this.

Line Dancing Lessons

Opportunities for future Community Involvement Programs discussed. Line dancing lessons nominated. Unanimous vote. We will do this again.

Meeting adjourned.

Bibliography

Hunters

Bakke, T. A. 1980. A revision of the family *Leucochloridiidae Poche* (Digenea) and studies on the morphology of *Leucochloridium paradoxum* Carus, 1835. *Systematic Parasitology* 1(3–4): 189–202.

Brusca, R. C., and M. R. Gilligan. 1983. Tongue replacement in a marine fish (*Lutjanus guttatus*) by a parasitic isopod (Crustacea: *Isopoda*). *Copeia* 1983(3): 813–816.

Chiou, T. H., S. Kleinlogel, T. Cronin, et al. 2008. Circular polarization vision in a stomatopod crustacean. *Current Biology* 18(6): 429–34.

Clark, R. J., J. Jensen, S. T. Nevin, B. P. Callaghan, et al. 2010. The engineering of an orally active conotoxin for the treatment of neuropathic pain. *Angewandte Chemie International Edition* 49(37): 6545–6548.

Cross, F. R., and R. R. Jackson. 2011. Olfaction-based anthropophily in a mosquito-specialist predator. *Biology Letters* 7(4): 510–512.

Cruz, L. J., W. R. Gray, and B. M. Olivera. 1978. Purification and properties of a myotoxin from *Conus geographus* venom. *Archives of Biochemistry and Biophysics* 190(2): 539–548.

Estók, P. S. Zsebők, and B. M. Siemers. 2009. Great tits search for, capture, kill and eat hibernating bats. *Biology Letters* 6: 59–62.

Feldman, D. H., B. M. Olivera, and D. Yoshikami. 1987. Omega *Conus geographus* toxin: A peptide that blocks calcium channels. *FEBS Letters* 214(2): 295–300.

Glover, C. N., C. Bucking, and C. M. Wood. 2011. Adaptations to *in situ* feeding: novel nutrient acquisition pathways in an ancient vertebrate. *Proceedings of the Royal Society B* 278(1721): 3096–3101.

Jackson, R. R., and X. J. Nelson. 2011. *Evarcha culicivora* chooses blood-fed *Anopheles* mosquitoes but other East African jumping spiders do not. *Medical and Veterinary Entomology* 26(2): 233–235.

Jackson, R. R., X. J. Nelson, and G. O. Sune. 2005. A spider that feeds indirectly on vertebrate blood by choosing female mosquitoes as prey. *Proceedings of the National Academy of Sciences* 102(42): 15155–15160.

Jen, Y. A. Lakhtakia, C. Yu, et al. 2011. Biologically inspired achromatic waveplates for visible light. *Nature Communications* 363(2): 1–5.

Patek, S. N., W. L. Korff, and R. L. Caldwell. 2004. Biomechanics: deadly strike mechanism of a mantis shrimp. *Nature* 428: 819–820.

Pekár, S., J. Šobotník, and Y. Lubin. 2011. Armoured spiderman: morphological and behavioural adaptations of a specialised araneophagous predator (Araneae: *Palpimanidae*). *Naturwissenschaften* 98(7): 593–603.

Ruffer, D. G. 1968. Agonistic behavior of the northern grasshopper mouse (*Onychomys leucogaster breviauritus*). *Journal of Mammalogy* 49(3): 481–487.

Salkeld, D. J., M. Salathé, P. Stapp, and J. H. Jones. 2010. Plague outbreaks in prairie dog populations explained by percolation thresholds of alternate host abundance. *Proceedings of the National Academy of Sciences* 107(32): 14247–14250.

Turner, P. S. 2005. Who you callin' shrimp? *National Wildlife* 43(6): 30.

Wesolowska, W., and R. R. Jackson. 2003. *Evarcha culicivora* sp. nov., a mosquito-eating jumping spider from East Africa (Araneae: *Salticidae*). *Annls zool Warsz* 53(2): 335–338.

Wignall, A. E., and P. W. Taylor. 2010. Predatory behaviour of an araneophagic assassin bug. *Journal of Ethology* 28(3): 437–445.

Wignall, A. E., and P. W. Taylor. 2011. Assassin bug uses aggressive mimicry to lure spider prey. *Proceedings of the Royal Society B* 278(1710): 1427–1433.

Wignall, A. E., R. R. Jackson, R. S. Wilcox, and P. W. Taylor. 2011. Exploitation of environmental noise by an araneophagic assassin bug. *Animal Behaviour* 82(5): 1037–1042.

Williams, S. H., E. Peiffer, and S. Ford. 2009. Gape and bite force in the rodents *Onychomys leucogaster* and *Peromyscus maniculatus*: does jaw muscle anatomy predict performance? *Journal of Morphology* 270(11): 1338–1347.

Wueringer, B. 2010. The sensory biology and feeding behaviour of sawfish. PhD Thesis, School of Biomedical Sciences, The University of Queensland.

Wueringer, B. E., L. Squire, and S. P. Collin. 2009. The biology of extinct and extant sawfish (Batoidea: Sclerorhynchidae and Pristidae). *Reviews in Fish Biology and Fisheries* 19(4): 445–464.

Wueringer, B. E., L. Squire, S. M. Kajiura, N. S. Hart, et al. 2012. The function of the sawfish's saw. *Current Biology* 22(5): 150–151.

Wueringer, B. E., S. C. Peverell, J. Seymour, L. Squire, et al. 2011. Sensory systems in sawfishes. 1. The ampullae of Lorenzini. *Brain Behavior and Evolution* 78(2): 139–149.

Zintzen, V., C. D. Roberts, M. J. Anderson, et al. 2011. Hagfish predatory behaviour and slime defence mechanism. *Scientific Reports* 1(31): 1–6.

Websites

Conus geographus Linnaeus 1758. *AELIUS_STILO@yahoo.com, penelope.uchicago.edu/~grout/encyclopaedia_romana/aconite/geographus.html* (accessed April 17, 2012).

Management of trade in freshwater sawfish under CITES. Department of Sustainability, Environment, Water, Population and Communities, *environment. gov.au/biodiversity/wildlife-trade/cites/ndf.html* (accessed April 17, 2012).

Rare tongue-eating parasite found. *BBC News, news.bbc.co.uk/2/hi/europe/ jersey/8246001.stm* (accessed April 17, 2012).

Cook, A. 2010. Primitive fish holds key to nylon replacement. *Cosmos Online, cosmosmagazine.com/news/3938/primitive-fish-holds-key-nylon-replacement* (accessed April 17, 2012).

Onion, Amanda. 2001.Tiny Shrimp Terrorizes Aquarium. ABC News Website, *abcnews.go.com/US/story?id=94488&page=1* (accessed May 29, 2012).

Seitz, J. C. FLMNH Ichthyology Department: Green Sawfish. *flmnh.ufl.edu/ fish/gallery/descript/greensawfish/greensawfish.htm* (accessed April 17, 2012).

PREY

Audubon, J. J. 1929. *Journal of John James Audubon: Made During His Trip to New Orleans in 1820–1821*. Cambridge, Massachusetts: The Business Historical Society.

Blackburn, D. C., J. Hanken, and F. A. Jenkins, Jr. 2008. Concealed weapons: erectile claws in African frogs. *Biology Letters* 4(4): 355–357.

Chazdon, R. L., and T. C. Whitmore. 2002. *Foundations of Tropical Forest Biology: Classic Papers With Commentaries*. Chicago: University of Chicago Press.

Cooper Jr., W. E. , Sherbrooke, W. C. 2010. Initiation of Escape Behavior by the Texas Horned Lizard (*Phrynosoma cornutum*) *Herpetologica* 66(1): 23–30.

Cooper Jr., W. E. and W. C. Sherbrooke. 2010. Plesiomorphic escape decisions in cryptic horned lizards (*Phrynosoma*) having highly derived antipredatory defenses. *Ethology* 116(10): 920–928.

Darwin, C. R. 1859. *On the Origin of Species.* Gillian Beer (ed.) New York: Oxford University Press, 2008.

Darwin, C. R. 1903. *More Letters of Charles Darwin: A Record of His Work in a Series of Hitherto Unpublished Letters, Volume 1.* Darwin, F., and A. C. Seward (eds.) London: John Murray.

Domínguez, M., L. V. Moreno, and S. B. Hedges. 2006. A new snake of the genus *Tropidophis* (Tropidophiidae) from the Guanahacabibes Peninsula of western Cuba. *Amphibia-Reptilia* 27(3): 427–432.

Dumbacher, J. P., B. M. Beehler, T. F. Spande, H. M. Garraffo, et al. 1992. Homobatrachotoxin in the genus *Pitohui*: chemical defense in birds? *Science* 258(5083): 799–801.

Dumbacher, J. P., A. Wako, S. R. Derrickson, A. Samuelson, et al. 2004. Melyrid beetles (*Choresine*): a putative source for the batrachotoxin alkaloids found in poison-dart frogs and toxic passerine birds. *Proceedings of the National Academy of Sciences* 101(45): 15857–15860.

Heiss, E., N. Natchev, D. Salaberger, M. Gumpenberger, et al. 2010. Hurt yourself to hurt your enemy: new insights on the function of the bizarre antipredator mechanism in the salamandrid *Pleurodeles waltl. Journal of Zoology* 280(2): 156–162.

Gabrielsen, G. W., and E. N. Smith. 2008. Physiological responses associated with feigned death in the American opossum. *Acta Physiologica Scandinavica* 123(4): 393–398.

Griffiths, R. A., P. T. Gregory, and L. A. Isaac. 2007. Death feigning by grass snakes (*Natrix natrix*) in response to handling by human "predators" *Journal of Comparative Psychology* 121(2): 123–129.

Jansal, S. A., and R. S. Voss. 2011. Adaptive evolution of the venom-targeted vWF protein in opossums that eat pitvipers. *PLoS ONE* 6(6): e20997.

Joron, M., L. Frezal, R. T. Jones, N. L. Chamberlain, et al. 2011. Chromosomal rearrangements maintain a polymorphic supergene controlling butterfly mimicry. *Nature* 477: 203–206.

Kingdon, J., B. Agwanda, M. Kinnaird, T. O'Brien, et al. 2011. A poisonous surprise under the coat of the African crested rat. *Proceedings of the Royal Society B* 279(1729): 675–680.

Marshall, L. G. 1988. Mammals and the Great American Interchange. *American Scientist* 76(4): 380.

Meijaarda, E., and G. de Silva Wijeyeratnec. 2010. Aquatic escape behaviour in mouse-deer provides insight into tragulid evolution. *Mammalian Biology— Zeitschrift für Säugetierkunde* 75(5): 471–473.

Middendorf III, G. A., and W. C. Sherbrooke. 1992. Canid elicitation of blood-squirting in a horned lizard (*Phrynosoma cornutum*). *Copeia* 1992(2): 519–527.

Middendorf III, G. A., W. C. Sherbrooke, and E. J. Braun. 2001. Comparison of blood squirted from the circumorbital sinus and systemic blood in a horned lizard, *Phrynosoma cornutum*. *The Southwestern Naturalist* 46(3): 384–387.

Mujica-Parodi, L. R., H. H. Strey, B. Frederick, R. Savoy, et al. Chemosensory cues to conspecific emotional stress activate amygdala in humans. *PLoS ONE* 4(7): e6415.

Müller, F. 1879. *Ituna* and *Thyridia*: a remarkable case of mimicry in butterflies. *Proceedings of the Entomological Society of London* 1879: 20–29.

Nilsson, D., E. J. Warrant, S. Johnsen, R. Hanlon, et al. 2012. A unique advantage for giant eyes in giant squid. *Current Biology* In Press, Corrected Proof, Available online March 15, 2012. *sciencedirect.com/science/article/pii/ S0960982212001820*.

Osborn, K. J., S. H. D. Haddock, F. Pleijel, L. P. Madin, et al. 2009. Deep-sea, swimming worms with luminescent "bombs." *Science* 325(5943): 964.

Osborn, K. J., L. P. Madin, and G. W. Rouse, 2010. The remarkable squidworm is an example of discoveries that await in deep-pelagic habitats. *Biology Letters* 7(3): 449–453.

Parejo, D., L. Amo, J. Rodríguez, and J. M. Avilés. 2012. Rollers smell the fear of nestlings. *Biology Letters* Published ahead of print March 7, 2012.

Ramsier, M. A., A. J. Cunningham, G. L. Moritz, J. J. Finneran, et al. 2012. Primate communication in the pure ultrasound. *Biology Letters* Published online before print February 8, 2012.

Sherbrooke, W. C., and G. A. Middendorf III. 2004. Responses of kit foxes (*Vulpes macrotis*) to antipredator blood-squirting and blood of Texas horned lizards (*Phrynosoma cornutum*). *Copeia* 3: 652–658.

Sherbrooke, W. C., and K. Schwen. 2008. Horned lizards (*Phrynosoma*) incapacitate dangerous ant prey with mucus. *Journal of Experimental Zoology Part A: Ecological Genetics and Physiology* 309A(8): 447–459.

Thewissen, J. G. M., L. N. Cooper, M. T. Clementz, S. Bajpai, et al. 2009.Whales originated from aquatic artiodactyls in the Eocene epoch of India. *Nature* 450: 1190–1194.

Wilson, A., C. L. Bonaparte, G. Ord, and W. M. Hetherington. 1831. *American Ornithology: Or the Natural History of the Birds of the United States, Volume 1.* (Google eBook) London: Constable and Co. Ltd.

Websites

Heying, Heather. 2003. Arthroleptidae. Animal Diversity Web, *animaldiversity .ummz.umich.edu/site/accounts/information/Arthroleptidae.html* (accessed April 17, 2012).

Walker, M. 2009. Pebble toad's rock and roll life. *BBC Earth News, news.bbc .co.uk/earth/hi/earth_news/newsid_8307000/8307333.stm* (accessed April 17, 2012).

Walker, M. 2011. Rapid venom evolution in pit vipers may be defensive. American Museum of Natural History, *eurekalert.org/pub_releases/2011–07/amon-rve 071811.php* (accessed April 17, 2012).

LOVERS AND FIGHTERS

Aitken-Palmer, C., R. Hou, C. Burrell, Z. Zhang, et al. 2012. Protracted reproductive seasonality in the male giant panda (*Ailuropoda melanoleuca*) reflected by patterns in androgen profiles, ejaculate characteristics, and selected behaviors. *Biology of Reproduction* Published online before print April 4, 2012, *biolreprod.org/content/early/2012/03/29/biolreprod.112.099044.*

Bartal, I. B., J. Decety, and P. Mason. 2011. Empathy and pro-social behavior in rats. *Science* 334(6061): 1427–1430.

Brennan, P. L. R., C. J. Clark, and R. O. Prum. 2010. Explosive eversion and functional morphology of the duck penis supports sexual conflict in waterfowl genitalia. *Proceedings of the Royal Society B* 277: 309–1314.

Brennan, P. L. R., R. O. Prum, K. G. McCracken, M. D. Sorenson, et al. 2007. Coevolution of male and female genital morphology in waterfowl. *PLoS ONE* 2(5): e418.

Feng, A. S., P. M. Narins, C. Xu, W. Lin, et al. 2006. Ultrasonic communication in frogs. *Nature* 440(7082): 333–336.

Grismer, J. L., and L. L. Grismer. 2010. Who's your mommy? Identifying maternal ancestors of asexual species of *Leiolepis* Cuvier, 1829 and the description of a new endemic species of asexual *Leiolepis* Cuvier, 1829 from southern Vietnam. *Zootaxa* 2433: 47–61.

Gwynne, D. T., and D. C. F. Rentz. 1983. Beetles on the bottle: male buprestids mistake stubbies for females (Coleoptera). *Australian Journal of Entomology* 22(1): 79–80.

Hawkeswood, T. J. 2005. Review of the biology and host-plants of the Australian jewel beetle *Julodimorpha bakewelli* (White, 1859) (Coleoptera: Buprestidae). *Calodema* 3: 3–5.

Jones, A. G., and N. L. Ratterman. 2009. Mate choice and sexual selection: what have we learned since Darwin? *Proceedings of the National Academy of Sciences* 6(Supplement 1): 10001–10008.

Kim, K. W. 2010. Synchronized contractive movement of *Amaurobius ferox* spiderlings. *Insectes Sociaux* 57(3): 323–332.

Lutes, A. A., D. P. Baumann, W. B. Neaves, and P. Baumann. 2011. Laboratory synthesis of an independently reproducing vertebrate species. *Proceedings of the National Academy of Sciences* 108(24): 9910–9915.

Lutes, A. A., W. B. Neaves, D. P. Baumann, W. Wiegraebe, and P. Baumann. 2010. Sister chromosome pairing maintains heterozygosity in parthenogenetic lizards. *Nature* 464: 283–286.

Medcalf, R. L. 2011. Desmoteplase: discovery, insights and opportunities for ischaemic stroke. *British Journal of Pharmacology* 165(1): 75–89.

Paczolt, K. A., and A. G. Jones. 2010. Post-copulatory sexual selection and sexual conflict in the evolution of male pregnancy. *Nature* 464: 401–404.

Phillips, K. A., C. A. Buzzell, N. Holder, and C. C. Sherwood. 2011. Why do capuchin monkeys urine wash? An experimental test of the sexual communication hypothesis using fMRI. *American Journal of Primatology* 73(6): 578–84.

Pietsch, T. W. 1975. Precocious sexual parasitism in the deep sea ceratioid anglerfish, *Cryptopsaras couesi* gill. *Nature* 256: 38–40.

Pietsch, T. W. 2005. Dimorphism, parasitism, and sex revisited: modes of reproduction among deep-sea ceratioid anglerfishes (Teleostei: Lophiiformes). *Ichthyological Research* 52: 207–236.

Rittmeyer, E. N., A. Allison, M. C. Gründler, and D. K. Thompson. 2012. Ecological guild evolution and the discovery of the world's smallest vertebrate. *PLoS ONE* 7(1): e29797.

Shen, J., A. S. Feng, Z. Xu, Z. Yu, et al. 2008. Ultrasonic frogs show hyperacute phonotaxis to female courtship calls. *Nature* 453: 914–916.

Shen, J., Z. Xu, Z. Yu, and S. Wang. 2011. Ultrasonic frogs show extraordinary sex differences in auditory frequency sensitivity. *Nature Communications* 2: 342.

Sueur, J., D. Mackie, and J. F. C. Windmill. 2011. So small, so loud: extremely high sound pressure level from a pygmy aquatic insect (*Corixidae, Micronectinae*). *PLoS ONE* 6(6): e21089.

Tan, M., G. Jones, G. Zhu, J. Ye, et al. 2009. Fellatio by fruit bats prolongs copulation time. *PLoS ONE* 4(10): e7595.

Xu, W., S. Wang, Z. Ouyang, J. Zhang, et al. 2009. Conservation of giant panda habitat in South Minshan, China, after the May 2008 earthquake. *Frontiers in Ecology and the Environment* 7: 353–358.

Zhang, X., C. Zhu, H. Lin, Q. Yang, et al. 2007. Wild fulvous fruit bats (*Rousettus leschenaulti*) exhibit human-like menstrual cycle. *Biology of Reproduction* 77(2): 358–364.

Websites

Fang, J. 2010. Male pipefish abort embryos of ugly mothers. *Nature News*, nature.com/news/2010/100317/full/news.2010.127.html (accessed April 17, 2012).

Graham, S. 2003. Vampire bat saliva compound could help treat strokes. *Scientific American*, scientificamerican.com/article.cfm?id=vampire-bat-saliva-compou (accessed April 17, 2012).

Handwerk, B. 2006. "Panda porn" to boost mating efforts at Thai zoo. *National Geographic News, news.nationalgeographic.com/news/2006/11/061113-panda-mate .html* (accessed April 17, 2012).

Kittiwongprom, S. 2007. Thai zoo tries more "panda porn" to foment lust. Reuters, *reuters.com/article/2007/03/27/us-thailand-pandas-attn-fahmy-idUS BKK10098320070327* (accessed April 17, 2012).

Randall, K. 2010. A Marine Mr Mom. Texas A&M University Marketing and Communications News Archive, *tamunews.tamu.edu/2010/03/17/a-marine-mr-mom* (accessed April 17, 2012).

Yates, D. 2008. Female concave-eared frogs draw mates with ultrasonic calls. University of Illinois News Bureau, *news.illinois.edu/news/08/0512frogs.html* (accessed April 17, 2012).

Yates, D. 2008. Ultrasonic frogs can tune their ears to different frequencies. University of Illinois News Bureau, *news.illinois.edu/news/08/0721frogears.html* (accessed April 17, 2012).

Pandas unexcited by Viagra. 2002. *BBC News, news.bbc.co.uk/2/hi/asia-pacific/ 2246588.stm* (accessed April 17, 2012).

Panda porn leads to baby bear boom. 2006. Associated Press, *theaustralian.com.au/ news/world/panda-porn-leads-to-baby-bear-boom/story-e6frg6so-1111112576858* (accessed April 17. 2012).

Odd Bodies

Becker, K. 1954. Pregnancy rates in two different samples of brown rats. *Journal of Mammalogy* 35(1): 119–121.

Burland, T. M., N. C. Bennett, J. R. M. Jarvis, and C. G. Faulkes. 2002. Eusociality in African mole-rats: new insights from patterns of genetic relatedness in the Damaraland mole-rat (*Cryptomys damarensis*). *Proceedings of the Royal Society B* 269(1495): 1025–1030.

Eeckhaut, I., E. Parmentier, P. Becker, S. Gomez da Silva, et al. 2004. Parasites and biotic diseases in field and cultivated sea cucumbers. FAO Fisheries Technical Paper 463: 311–325.

Larson, J., and T. J. Park. 2009. Extreme hypoxia tolerance of naked mole-rat brain. *NeuroReport* 20(18): 1634–1637.

Lea, A. M. 1916. Notes on the Lord Howe Island phasma, and on an associated longicorn beetle. *Proceedings of the Royal Society of South Australia* 40: 145–147.

Meehan, C. J., E. J. Olson, M. W. Reudink, T. K. Kyser, et al. 2009. Herbivory in a spider through exploitation of an ant–plant mutualism. *Current Biology* 19(19): 892–893.

Meyer-Rochow, V. B. 1977. Comparison between 15 *Carapus mourlani* in a single holothurian and 19 *C. mourlani* from starfish. *Copeia* 1977(3): 582–584.

Meyer-Rochow, V. B. 1979. Stomach and gut contents of *Carapus mourlani* from starfish and a holothurian. *Ann. Zool. Fennici* 16: 287–289.

Osborn, K. J., G. W. Rouse, S. K. Goffredi, and B. H. Robison. 2007. Description and relationships of *Chaetopterus pugaporcinus*, an unusual pelagic polychaete (Annelida, Chaetopteridae). *The Biological Bulletin* 212(1): 40–54.

Park, T. J., Y. Lu, R. Jüttner, E. Smith, et al. 2008. Selective inflammatory pain insensitivity in the African naked mole-rat (*Heterocephalus glaber*). *PLoS Biol* 6(1): e13.

Priddel, D., N. Carlile, M. Humphrey, S. Fellenberg, and D. Hiscox. 2003. Rediscovery of the "extinct" Lord Howe Island stick-insect (*Dryococelus australis* [Montrouzier]) (Phasmatodea) and recommendations for its conservation. *Biodiversity and Conservation* 12(7): 1391–1403.

Roellig, K., B. Drews, F. Goeritz, and T. B. Hildebrandt. 2011. The long gestation of the small naked mole-rat (*Heterocephalus glaber* RüPPELL, 1842) studied with ultrasound biomicroscopy and 3D-ultrasonography. *PLoS ONE* 6(3): e17744.

Schütz, D., and M. Taborsky. 2003. Adaptations to an aquatic life may be responsible for the reversed sexual size dimorphism in the water spider, *Argyroneta aquatica*. *Evolutionary Ecology Research* 5: 105–117.

Seymour, R. S., and S. K. Hetz. 2011. The diving bell and the spider: the physical gill of *Argyroneta aquatica*. *Journal of Experimental Biology* 214: 2175–2181.

St. John Smith, E., D. Omerbašić, S. G. Lechner, and G. Anirudhan. 2011. The molecular basis of acid insensitivity in the African naked mole-rat. *Science* 334(6062): 1557–1560.

Strohm, E. 2010. How can cleptoparasitic drosophilid flies emerge from the closed brood cells of the red mason bee? *Physiological Entomology* 36(1): 77–83.

van der Horst, G., L. Maree, S. H. Kotzé, and M. J. O'Riain. 2011. Sperm structure and motility in the eusocial naked mole-rat, *Heterocephalus glaber*: a case of degenerative orthogenesis in the absence of sperm competition? *BMC Evolutionary Biology* 11: 351.

Whitehead, A., F. Galvez, S. Zhang, L. M. Williams, et al. 2011. Functional genomics of physiological plasticity and local adaptation in killifish. *Journal of Heredity* 102(5): 499–511.

Websites

Common mummichog. Gulf of Maine Research Institute, *gma.org/fogm/Fundulus_heteroclitus.htm* (accessed April 17, 2012).

Dryococelus australis in Species Profile and Threats Database. 2012. Department of Sustainability, Environment, Water, Population and Communities, *environment.gov.au/sprat* (accessed April 12. 2012).

Engber, D. 2011. The Mouse Trap. *Slate, slate.com/articles/health_and_science/the_mouse_trap/2011/11/the_mouse_trap.html* (accessed April 17, 2012).

Fulton-Bennett, K. 2007. A worm like no other. Monterey Bay Aquarium Research Institute Press Room, *mbari.org/news/homepage/2007/pworm.html* (accessed April 17, 2012).

Genova, C. 2009. First "mainly vegetarian" spider described. Cell Press, *eurekalert.org/pub_releases/2009-10/cp-fv100509.php* (accessed April 17. 2012).

Rouge, M. 2003. Sperm motility. *Pathophysiology of the Reproductive System,* Colorado State University hypertextbook, *vivo.colostate.edu/hbooks/pathphys/reprod/semeneval/motility.html* (accessed April 17, 2012).

Segelken, R. 1999. Counting mole-rat mammaries and hungry pups, biologists explain why naked rodents break the rules. *Cornell News, news.cornell.edu/releases/Aug99/rat_mamm.hrs.html* (accessed April 17, 2012).

Summerlin, L. B. (ed.) SP-401 Skylab, Classroom in Space. George C. Marshall Space Flight Center, *history.nasa.gov/SP-401/ch17.htm* (accessed April 17, 2012).

ANCIENT CREATURES

Carney, R. M., J. Vinther, M. D. Shawkey, L. D'Alba, and J. Ackermann. 2012. New evidence on the colour and nature of the isolated *Archaeopteryx* feather. *Nature Communications* 3 Article number 637.

Gianechini, F. A., F. L. Agnolín, and M. D. Ezcurra. 2010. A reassessment of the purported venom delivery system of the bird-like raptor *Sinornithosaurus*. *Paläontologische Zeitschrift* 85: 103–107.

Gonga, E., L. D. Martin, D. A. Burnhamb, and A. R. Falk. 2009. The birdlike raptor *Sinornithosaurus* was venomous. *Proceedings of the National Academy of Sciences* 107(2): 766–768.

Kundrát, M., and J. Janácek. 2007. Cranial pneumatization and auditory perceptions of the oviraptorid dinosaur *Conchoraptor gracilis* (Theropoda, Maniraptora) from the Late Cretaceous of Mongolia. *Die Naturwissenschaften* 94(9): 769–778.

Li1, Q., K. Gao, Q. Meng, J. A. Clarke, et al. 2012. Reconstruction of *Microraptor* and the evolution of iridescent plumage. *Science* 335(6073): 1215–1219.

Peterson, J. E., M. D. Henderson, R. P. Scherer, and C. P. Vittore. 2009. Face biting on a juvenile Tyrannosaurid and behavioural implications. *Palaios* 24: 780–784.

Quintana, J., M. Köhler, S. Moyà-Solà. 2011. *Nuralagus rex*, gen. et sp. nov., an endemic insular giant rabbit from the Neogene of Minorca (Balearic Islands, Spain). *Journal of Vertebrate Paleontology* 31: 231–240.

Schmitz, L., and R. Motani. 2011. Nocturnality in dinosaurs inferred from scleral ring and orbit morphology. *Science* 332(6030): 705–708.

Secord, R., J. I. Bloch, S. G. B. Chester, and D. M. Boyer. 2012. Evolution of the earliest horses driven by climate change in the Paleocene-Eocene Thermal Maximum. *Science* 335(6071): 959–962.

Williams, S. H., E. Peiffer, and S. Ford. 2009. Gape and bite force in the rodents *Onychomys leucogaster* and *Peromyscus maniculatus*: does jaw-muscle anatomy predict performance? *Journal of Morphology* 270(11): 1338–1347.

Wolff, E. D. S., S. W. Salisbury, J. R. Horner, and D. J. Varricchio. 2009. Common avian infection plagued the tyrant dinosaurs. *PLoS ONE* 4(9): e7288.

Xu, X., K. Wang, K. Zhang, Q. Ma, et al. 2012. A gigantic feathered dinosaur from the Lower Cretaceous of China. *Nature* 484: 92–95.

Websites

Giant Extinct Rabbit was the King of Minorca. 2011. Giant Extinct Rabbit was the King of Minorca, *vertpaleo.org/source/blog/post.cfm/press-release-giant-extinct-rabbit-was-the-king-of-minorca* (accessed April 5, 2012).

Index

About the Author

BECKY CREW GREW UP in the Blue Mountains of New South Wales with, variously, a dog, cats, rabbits, quails, rats, a homing pigeon, and some mice she hid from her parents. She hated science in school, eschewing cells, ribosomes, and chemical equations to study Classical and Near Eastern archaeology at the University of Sydney, paying the bills by working in the finance sector. The machinations of the finance world failed to satisfy her innate fascination with animals, so she started the blog *Running Ponies* as a creative outlet with her friend Sara. *Running Ponies* led to Becky being named Australian Science Blogger of the Year in 2010. Becky's enthusiasm for science writing led to her next role as Online Editor at Australian science magazine *COSMOS*. Becky has appeared on national Australian radio to discuss the best, worst, and weirdest the animal world has to offer, has spoken at various conferences, has had *Running Ponies* invited into the *Scientific American* Blog Network, and has battled intense desires for naps and snacks to release this, her first book. Although she is content with her tuxedo-wearing cat Bailey and oversized sea snails, her dream is to one day have her very own seagull—the most smartly dressed of all the sea birds.